Kobe Bryant

by John F. Wukovits

LUCENT BOOKS
A part of Gale, Cengage Learning

GALE
CENGAGE Learning™

Detroit • New York • San Francisco • New Haven, Conn • Waterville, Maine • London

© 2011 Gale, Cengage Learning

LIBRARY OF CONGRESS CATALOGING-IN-PUBLICATION DATA

Wukovits, John F., 1944-
Kobe Bryant / by John F. Wukovits.
    p. cm. -- (People in the news)
Includes bibliographical references and index.
ISBN 978-1-4205-0593-1 (hardcover)
1. Bryant, Kobe, 1978- 2. Basketball players--United States--Biography.
3. Los Angeles Lakers (Basketball team) I. Title.
GV884.B794W85 2011
796.323092--dc22
  [B]
                                                                2011003741

Lucent Books
27500 Drake Rd.
Farmington Hills, MI 48331

ISBN-13: 978-1-4205-0593-1
ISBN-10: 1-4205-0593-9

Printed in the United States of America
 2 3 4 5 6 7 15 14 13 12 11
Printed by Bang Printing, Brainerd, MN, 2nd Ptg., 06/2011

Contents

F ame and celebrity are alluring. People are drawn to those who walk in fame's spotlight, whether they are known for great accomplishments or for notorious deeds. The lives of the famous pique public interest and attract attention, perhaps because their experiences seem in some ways so different from, yet in other ways so similar to, our own.

Newspapers, magazines, and television regularly capitalize on this fascination with celebrity by running profiles of famous people. For example, television programs such as *Entertainment Tonight* devote all of their programming to stories about entertainment and entertainers. Magazines such as *People* fill their pages with stories of the private lives of famous people. Even newspapers, newsmagazines, and television news frequently delve into the lives of well-known personalities. Despite the number of articles and programs, few provide more than a superficial glimpse at their subjects.

Lucent's People in the News series offers young readers a deeper look into the lives of today's newsmakers, the influences that have shaped them, and the impact they have had in their fields of endeavor and on other people's lives. The subjects of the series hail from many disciplines and walks of life. They include authors, musicians, athletes, political leaders, entertainers, entrepreneurs, and others who have made a mark on modern life and who, in many cases, will continue to do so for years to come.

These biographies are more than factual chronicles. Each book emphasizes the contributions, accomplishments, or deeds that have brought fame or notoriety to the individual and shows how that person has influenced modern life. Authors portray their subjects in a realistic, unsentimental light. For example, Bill Gates—the cofounder and chief executive officer of the software giant Microsoft—has been instrumental in making personal computers the most vital tool of the modern age. Few dispute his business savvy, his perseverance, or his technical expertise, yet critics say he is ruthless in his dealings with competitors and driven more by his desire to maintain Microsoft's dominance in the computer industry than by an interest in furthering technology.

In these books, young readers will encounter inspiring stories about real people who achieved success despite enormous obstacles. Oprah Winfrey—the most powerful, most watched, and wealthiest woman on television today—spent the first six years of her life in the care of her grandparents while her unwed mother sought work and a better life elsewhere. Her adolescence was colored by rape, pregnancy at age fourteen, and sexual abuse.

Each author documents and supports his or her work with an array of primary and secondary source quotations taken from diaries, letters, speeches, and interviews. All quotes are footnoted to show readers exactly how and where biographers derive their information and provide guidance for further research. The quotations enliven the text by giving readers eyewitness views of the life and accomplishments of each person covered in the People in the News series.

In addition, each book in the series includes photographs, annotated bibliographies, timelines, and comprehensive indexes. For both the casual reader and the student researcher, the People in the News series offers insight into the lives of today's newsmakers—people who shape the way we live, work, and play in the modern age.

A Boy's Dream

From the time he was a young boy, Kobe Bryant exhibited amazing talent on the basketball court, skills that impressed onlookers and made some of them comment that he had a future as a professional athlete. While most elementary school students grappled with the typical woes and joys of being a child—grades, acceptance, friendship, first girlfriend or boyfriend—Bryant could be found in front of a backboard, launching golden arcs with a basketball or dribbling around and through imaginary opponents.

"From day one, I was dribbling," Bryant told *Slam* magazine, a publication devoted to covering every aspect of basketball. "I just found basketball to be the most fun. It was the fact that you could dribble the ball around everywhere. You could play the game by yourself and envision certain situations."[1] The basketball court became Bryant's kingdom, a realm he controlled like a wizard and a world in which he was the star.

The feeling intensified for the six-year-old Bryant when his father moved the family to Italy for seven years, a change that further isolated a youth who had to deal with a new country, unfamiliar language, and different customs. With his personal world altering in leaps and bounds, Bryant clutched more tightly to the one constant, the one area he knew would never change—the basketball court.

He spent hours practicing his jump shot or his ball-handling skills, pretending he held the ball in the final seconds with the game's outcome on the line. A series of basketball greats that he admired served as his imaginary foes—Earvin "Magic" Johnson of the Los Angeles Lakers and Larry Bird from the Boston Celtics most often materialized—but none could halt the elementary school student from snatching victory as the clock ran out. Numerous times, Kobe Bryant pretended to hold the National Basketball Association's championship trophy in one hand and the Most Valuable Player trophy in the other, symbolizing greatness that few had ever achieved in the professional game.

As a boy Kobe dreamed of playing with basketball greats like Los Angeles Laker Earvin "Magic" Johnson and Boston Celtic Larry Bird.

In the United States, he could readily find a group of boys and engage in a game of pickup basketball, but Italian youngsters gravitated to that nation's most popular sport—soccer. Basketball in hand, Bryant headed to the court hoping to find a few classmates ready to play but knowing that he would most likely be playing alone while the other boys ran off to the soccer field. For young Kobe Bryant, the team sport of basketball became an individual pursuit, with the game and opponents unfolding in his imagination as his talented hands directed the ball and launched game-winning shots.

Bryant's solitary pursuit was a double-edged sword, however. The long hours practicing alone sharpened his skills and made him more ready to compete in tougher situations, but at the same time it hardened his isolation. When he returned to the United States to play high school basketball, Bryant brought the same approach to the team sport that he had employed on the practice courts in Italy—he was the star who would bring home victory when everyone else stumbled.

Those competing themes—individual excellence versus team play—dominated and frustrated Kobe Bryant's life. Because he had put in so many hours of practice, he could do things on the basketball court that few fellow players thought of attempting, yet he had to stifle a desire to dominate games for the good of the team. It is a struggle that still exists, and one that Bryant will probably never completely resolve, but in the attempt to find a proper balance between the two, Kobe Bryant has found true excellence.

Chapter 1

Origins of a Champion

It is not surprising that Kobe Bryant developed a love for basketball. His father played in the National Basketball Association (NBA). However, Kobe's early life offered twists and turns not often tossed at six- and seven-year-old children. Those challenges helped mold the young Kobe Bryant into the athlete he is today, but in the process, they planted attitudes and outlooks that created turmoil.

Life Overseas

Kobe Bryant was born August 23, 1978, in Philadelphia, Pennsylvania. His parents, Joe and Pamela, named their son after a much-esteemed Japanese delicacy called kobe beef.

His father was a high school basketball star in Philadelphia in the early 1970s who became one of the first athletes to forgo college and advance directly to the professional ranks. The 6-foot-9-inch forward (205.74cm) possessed remarkably gifted ball-handling talents for a large man, and in 1976 he became a member of his hometown team, the Philadelphia 76ers. Joe Bryant had money and talent, and he played before an adoring fan base.

After eight mediocre seasons in the NBA, Bryant signed a contract to play professional ball in Italy. In 1984, he and Pamela, accompanied by eight-year-old daughter Sharia, seven-year-old daughter Shaya, and six-year-old Kobe, purchased a home

Kobe's father, Philadelphia 76ers Joe "Jellybean" Bryant, shoots over Milwaukee's Kent Benson. Joe was a high school basketball star who became one of the first athletes to forgo college and advance directly to the NBA.

in Rieti, a town of forty thousand people in central Italy. The sudden change in culture, language, and customs almost proved too traumatic for the young boy, who felt isolated at school at a time when youngsters need a stable base and an array of friends. "It was difficult at first because I couldn't speak Italian," he said. "So my two sisters and I got together after school to teach each other the words we had learned. I was able to speak Italian pretty well within a few months."[2]

At the same time, the sense of existing in his own world taught Kobe a valuable lesson—if he were to survive, he had to handle matters on his own. "I was six when we moved there and I had to pick up a whole new language, plus my parents threw us into an all-Italian school, so it was sink or swim,"[3] he says. In facing the situation, Kobe gained a self-confidence that he could deal with problems without resorting to help from outsiders.

He was more than happy to accept advice and support from his family, however. Living in a different country and being one of only a few black families in the region caused the Bryants to turn to each other, and the tight-knit family helped each other adapt to European ways. "We really began to rely heavily on each other because we were all we had,"[4] said his older sister Sharia of their time in Italy.

The Bryants agreed, though, that despite the difficulties first experienced, Italy offered much they liked. Italians placed great emphasis on family, and the Bryants felt fully welcomed into Italian culture. Everyone appeared to be treated as equals. "They don't mistrust each other," explained Kobe. "They say hello when they see you on the street. And family—family is big there."[5] The children grew accustomed to seeing extended families, including grandparents, living in one home, and the Bryants enjoyed long dinners together, sharing good food and laughter for hours. Kobe's sojourn in the country so impressed him that he often takes summer vacations in that nation.

Practicing His Game

Loving basketball in a soccer-crazed country set Kobe apart from his fellow students. While he lofted shot after shot at the hoop his father had erected in the backyard, most boys his age rushed to the soccer field. "After school I would be the only guy on the basketball court, working on my moves, and then kids would start showing up with their soccer ball," he explained. "I could hold them off if there were two or three of them, but when they got to be 11 or 12, I had to give up the court. It was either go home or be the goalkeeper."[6]

Hour after hour, Kobe worked on his game, honing jump shots and drives to the basket. His classmates taunted him that while he might be a good player in Italy, when he returned to the United States he would be no better than average. The harsh words hurt Kobe but made him more determined to succeed when given the chance.

He returned to Philadelphia at the end of each school year to participate in summer basketball leagues, and the experience made him wonder whether his Italian classmates had a point. He had enough talent that by the time he entered sixth grade, he was competing against athletes from high school, and while flattering, those contests opened his eyes to the fact that he had a way to go before being considered a superb player. During that entire summer before sixth grade, Kobe failed to score even a single basket.

"Zero. Not one point," he said. "So that winter, back in Italy, I just worked on my game and came back the following year a better player." He added, "That experience really propelled me,"[7] as it taught him that only through hard work and constant repetition could he become the player he hoped to be.

Family Help

Not surprisingly, Kobe turned to family for help on the court. As he slowly adjusted to life overseas, his father became one of the most popular basketball stars in Italy, tossing in baskets at the rate of 30 points per game. Fans chanted his name when he scored, and newspapers claimed he was better than Earvin "Magic" Johnson or any other acclaimed NBA talent. If his team triumphed in an important game, Joe Bryant knew he would not

An eleven-year-old Bryant challenged Brian Shaw, a first-round NBA draft pick playing in Italy, to play a game of H-O-R-S-E. The young Kobe was challenging grown men to play one-on-one, and he really thought he could win.

have to pay for a meal for the remainder of the week—fans or restaurant owners happily picked up the tab.

Kobe studied his father to understand what made him a good player, then tried to copy his moves on the court. Joe taught his son how to dribble with either hand, how to fake an opponent into moving one way while he went a different path to the basket, and how to play defense. Above all, Joe emphasized that Kobe should enjoy himself and love what he was doing. "My father always played with a great love for the game, and that's one thing he always taught me," Kobe said. "He told me not to let the pressure or the expectations take away from my love for the game. I think that's the best advice anyone's ever given me."[8]

Father and son scrutinized videotapes of NBA games sent by Kobe's grandparents from back home or from scouting services that offered taped games for purchase. Joe pointed out how Kareem Abdul-Jabbar positioned himself to snare rebounds, or told his son to watch how Larry Bird shook free of his defender to go in for an easy layup. Kobe recalled later, "My father told me, 'Watch this. See this guy? This is how you can make use of your left hand.'"[9]

As Kobe followed along, Joe would seemingly predict the moves each athlete employed or where the ball would end up. He explained that an opponent often gives clues as to what he is about to do in how he moves his shoulders, hands, and feet or whether he leans slightly to one side or the other. Kobe watched the games over and over and became so familiar with the techniques of Magic Johnson and other top players that he knew what they were about to do before they did it. Kobe stated that he learned the fall-away jump shot by studying Hakeem Olajuwon, how to feint one way and quickly dart another from Earl "the Pearl" Monroe, and his baseline jump shot from Hall of Fame guard Oscar Robertson.

Joe even took Kobe to some of his basketball practices so he could learn firsthand how professionals play the game. He often shot baskets at one end of the court while his dad practiced at the other, and even sometimes stepped onto the home court at halftime to shoot around until the teams returned from the locker rooms. "The crowd would be cheering me on," Kobe recalled. "I loved it."[10]

Magic Johnson

Before becoming an NBA star himself, Kobe Bryant's favorite NBA team was the Los Angeles Lakers, and his favorite star was Lakers great Magic Johnson. He taped a large poster of the noted guard to his bedroom wall in Italy and hoped one day to imitate Johnson's wizardry on the basketball court. Bryant's dream was to play for the same team, the Lakers, and lead them to championships the way Johnson had done.

In November 1991, the family learned that Kobe's idol had suddenly retired from basketball due to an illness. Johnson had tested positive for HIV, an infection that in those days usually resulted in death. Rather than continue to compete, which might endanger fellow players, Johnson left the game he so loved.

The event mortified Kobe Bryant, who had assumed his hero would last forever. "I was sad because Kobe was sad," his sister Sharia said. "I never imagined feeling that way about somebody I'd never met. It hurt him as if it was a family member. For a week he was missing meals. It was really, really hard for him."

Quoted in Ian Thomsen. "Showtime!." *Sports Illustrated*, April 27, 1998. http://sports illustrated.cnn.com/vault/article/magazine/MAG1012689/index.htm.

Kobe was devastated after he learned that his idol Earvin "Magic" Johnson had suddenly retired from basketball after testing positive for HIV.

Kobe became a fixture at his father's games and practices, and he improved so much that as he grew older he wanted to challenge some of his father's teammates. Some would oblige and embark on one-on-one games with Kobe, going at half speed or pretending to fall down as Kobe moved to the basket. One day, the eleven-year-old Kobe kept pleading with Brian Shaw, a first-round NBA draft pick playing in Italy due to a contract dispute, to play a game of H-O-R-S-E. Shaw let Kobe win, but he noticed something different in the young boy.

"To this day Kobe claims he beat me," says Shaw. "I'm like, 'Right, [I'm really trying to beat] an 11-year-old kid.' But he's serious. His dad was a good player, but he was the opposite of Kobe, real laid-back. Kobe was out there challenging grown men to play one-on-one, and he really thought he could win."[11]

Along the way, Kobe, who always had the basic skills to be elite in basketball, picked up additional moves and shots, which he honed until they became his own. Constant repetition on the practice court and hours studying the game's greats turned him into a youth who could handily dominate any game in which he played. "Kobe has always been a very creative young man," said Joe. "I saw him jump off a gymnastic springboard to propel himself for a reverse dunk when he was eight years old. That's when I knew he'd be special ... different, whether it was basketball, football, soccer, or whatever."[12]

Kobe Bryant was ready to take his game back to the United States.

To High School

The Bryants returned to Pennsylvania in the summer of 1991, settling in Lower Merion, a wealthy suburb of Philadelphia. Kobe enrolled at Bala Cynwyd Junior High School and unexpectedly experienced the same difficulties fitting in as he had in Italy. Though he was back in his home country, he had been away for most of his life, knew more about Italian customs than American ones, spoke English with an Italian accent, and was black in a largely white school.

"It was tough because I didn't know English really well, and I really didn't know the different lingo that black culture had," Bryant explained. "So I had to learn two languages when I got back here, and that was tough. But if I didn't do it, I would have never fit in. And kids are tough, you know? You got to be just like them or else."[13]

As always, when facing unsettled conditions elsewhere, Bryant turned to the basketball court, the one world he controlled and in which he could be king. Almost every day, he jogged to a park near his suburban Philadelphia home and shot hundreds of baskets, practicing twists and turns and banking layups until such matters became second nature. "That's where I would dream of hitting game-winning shots and winning NBA championships,"[14] Bryant later claimed.

He joined a noted summer league in Philadelphia to pit his talent against the area's best and came away with the realization that while he had much work yet to do, he could hold his own against players a few years older than he was. He became so convinced that the NBA awaited him that he listed professional basketball as his future career on a summer camp form. A counselor scoffed at the idea. "The guy said NBA players are one in a million," Bryant recalled. "I said, 'Man, look, I'm going to be that one in a million.' You see Magic, Michael [Jordan]— they made it. What's different about them?"[15] The incident only made him more determined to make it, no matter what anyone else thought.

The eighth grader's wizardry on the court soon caught the attention of Gregg Downer, the varsity coach at Lower Merion High School. In an effort to learn more about the youngster, Downer invited Bryant to scrimmage against his varsity, which included more developed and muscular players who were four years older than Bryant. "Here's this kid, and he has no fear of us at all," said Doug Young, then a sophomore. "He's throwing elbows, setting hard screens."[16]

Downer immediately knew that something special awaited his team at Lower Merion High. "I had invited him to scrimmage against our varsity," said Downer, "and after five minutes of play I turned to my assistant coaches and said, 'This guy's a pro.'"[17]

Despite a horrid team record of 4-20, Bryant showed flashes of greatness in his freshman year under Downer, leading the team in scoring with 18 points a game. Downer noticed that his budding star did not merely possess the necessary talent to play at a top level but had the willingness to outwork everyone else. "I've seen a lot of high school basketball, but I have never seen anyone as good as Kobe was," Downer recalled. "He had such enormous potential. You could see that right away. He also had a great work ethic and a tremendous desire to succeed, which is something you don't often see in kids that age."[18]

Bryant continued his hard work during the summer, lifting weights and jumping rope in an effort to become stronger and more agile. He hoped that his efforts, which included joining summer leagues and scrimmaging against his father, would produce better results in his sophomore year.

An Improving Athlete

They did. Downer emphasized team play at the start of the season and cautioned that anyone who did not buy into that concept would spend a lot of time on the bench. He asked for a game that concentrated on moving the ball around until a player broke free, then getting the ball to that man for an open shot. Bryant followed his coach's wishes, but also hoped he could show that the team could depend on him in tight spots. "Why would you even play if you didn't want to be the best player who ever lived?" asked Bryant. "That's how I would think everyone would go into it. You want to be the man, you know, not the best of the moment, but the best who ever set foot on a basketball court."[19]

Bryant averaged 22 points and 10 rebounds in his sophomore year in helping his team improve to 16-6, a record that earned them a spot in the playoffs. After winning in the first round, Lower Merion bowed out in the second, but relying on Bryant's stellar play, they were a team on the rise.

"He had a focus and concentration that is completely rare for any kid, but that's what made his game so good," said Downer. At the same time, Bryant displayed an ego that did not quite match Downer's emphasis on the team aspect. The basketball court "was his world and he was the king, and he let you know it in no uncertain terms,"[20] stated one of his former teammates at Lower Merion.

A Maturing Bryant

Bryant managed to squeeze some fun into his life, but even that often centered around basketball. Jocelyn Ebron, whom the seventeen-year-old met in 1995 at a barbecue, was attracted to

Brandy

Jocelyn Ebron may have been Bryant's first girlfriend, but as his fame grew, so too did his popularity. Ebron gained firsthand knowledge of that when, to her surprise, Bryant asked another girl to the senior prom—noted singer Brandy—whom Bryant had met at an awards show. "He told me that his agent wanted him to ask Brandy because it would help him gain attention," says Ebron. "I was hurt, but he said it was for the best, so I had to accept that."

Photographers captured every moment of the date, including when the couple left Bryant's home after spending time with his parents. They danced and laughed at the prom and appeared to enjoy the evening, but neither star felt entirely comfortable. Bryant was more at home with his basketball videotapes or with a backyard hoop, and the outgoing Brandy preferred wilder times over calm evenings. As a friend of hers said, "He wasn't this wild guy who wanted to do fun things. He'd lived in this cocoon provided by his family. Brandy liked to live life."

Quoted in Allison Samuels. "Kobe Off the Court." *Newsweek*, October 13, 2003. www.newsweek.com/2003/10/12/kobe-off-the-court.html.

Bryant's calm manner and quietness that bordered on shyness. Most boys she knew boasted of all the girlfriends they knew, but Bryant seemed to care only for her—and basketball.

Ebron quickly realized that basketball was Bryant's whole life. Rather than going to a movie or the local teenage hangout, Bryant instead brought out videotapes of his games or of NBA contests. "He wanted to watch them all the time," explained Ebron. "I didn't mind, because I wanted to do what he wanted to do. Looking back, it was sort of selfish of him."[21]

His family encouraged this attitude by making Bryant the center of attention. His father attended every game, and Ebron noticed that even his sisters accepted that their brother, as the parents' only son and basketball star, would be king at home.

As a junior, Bryant averaged 31 points and 10 rebounds in leading the team to a 26-5 record. After capturing the Central League championship, Lower Merion advanced to the second round of the state playoffs before losing to Hazelton, 64-59. Despite registering 33 points and 15 rebounds in that loss, after the game Bryant apologized to his teammates for not performing better and promised he would do everything he could to bring home a state title in his senior year. "The work starts now,"[22] he added.

During the summer and into his senior year, Bryant scheduled morning workouts from 5:00 to 7:00 A.M. to improve his game. Now gaining attention as one of the nation's top talents, Bryant received invitations to attend the most prestigious summer basketball camps. He competed in a tournament of the best athletes, held in Las Vegas, and was named the most valuable player at another camp sponsored by Adidas.

Even professionals took notice. During the summer between his junior and senior year, Bryant received permission to work out with the Philadelphia 76ers. Though he obviously did not possess the same skill level, he held his own in occasional games of one-on-one, at times coming close to defeating his opponent.

Honors Pour In

Bryant opened his senior basketball season intent on bringing a state title to Lower Merion. He had grown to 6 feet 6 inches

Kobe helped his team to another triumph in a hard-fought 60-53 defeat of bitter rival Chester High School, which had beaten Merion by 27 points the year before.

(198.12cm) and had added another 15 pounds (6.8kg) since his freshman year, and college scouts attending his games expected him to back up his hopes. When the team stumbled and lost three of its first seven games, however, Downer told his squad they had been playing as individuals instead of as a team and that anyone who could not put individual honors aside should hand in his uniform.

No one did. Bryant so increased his focus that even in practice the other players stood in awe. He took everything, even three-against-three scrimmages, as a challenge. When teammate Rob Schwartz missed an easy basket during a scrimmage tied at 9, allowing the other trio to win, Bryant pursued Schwartz into the hallway to scold him. An astonished Schwartz stood as Bryant chewed him out as if they had just lost the state championship.

In an effort to help his teammates improve, Bryant persuaded them to stay after practice for more work. They engaged in bitterly contested games of one-on-one up to 100 points, clashes Bryant took personally. In one match, Bryant scored 80 points before Schwartz registered his first basket, and Schwartz contended that the best he ever did against Bryant was lose 100-12.

The increased focus turned the team around as Lower Merion recorded twenty-seven straight wins in a steady march to the state championship. Bryant garnered so much attention that he had to hire a public-relations person to keep track of the hundreds of requests for interviews from various state and national media outlets. "Traveling with Kobe was like traveling with a rock star,"[23] said Downer.

The team waltzed into the playoffs. Bryant scored 50 points in a 95-68 win in a quarterfinal game against Academy Park High School, then helped his team to another triumph in a hard-fought 60-53 defeat of bitter rival Chester High School, which had beaten Merion by 27 points the year before. Bryant and his teammates wore the number 27 on their warm-up jerseys before the game as a reminder of what had occurred a year earlier.

In the next game, against Cedar Cliff High School, Merion was trailing by 8 points late in the first half when Bryant changed the momentum. In a play that called for a pass to Bryant, the passer tossed the ball a little behind Bryant. Almost without pause, Bryant grabbed the ball with his left hand, turned toward the basket while in the air, and slammed home a massive dunk shot that had fans cheering and the opponents speechless. Sparked by what Downer called the best dunk he had ever seen, Merion went on to score the next 12 points and win the game.

One day before the state semifinal, Bryant broke his nose during practice. Now so close to his goal of capturing a state title, Bryant would not let the injury hold him back. The team fashioned a mask to give Bryant some protection for his fragile nose, but once the game arrived, Bryant had nothing to do with it. "Kobe had the mask on in warm-ups, and he came into the locker room right before the game was ready to start, ripped the mask off, threw it against the wall and said, 'Let's go play,'" Downer recalled. "That was an example of how physically and how mentally tough he is. He played the last two games with a broken nose, and we were probably one well-placed elbow back then from having our state championship dreams con to an end."[24]

Broken nose and all, Bryant scored 12 points in the fourth quarter to bring his team from the brink of defeat to tie the game in regulation, and then added 8 more points in overtime for a 77-69 win. Three nights later, they played Erie Cathedral Preparatory School for the Class AAAA title. As opposing fans jeered what they called an overrated Bryant, Erie darted to a 21-15 halftime lead, holding Bryant to 8 points. Merion came out for the second half with a flurry, scoring 11 straight points to open up a slim lead along the way to a 47-43 victory and the state championship. Bryant joined his teammates in climbing a ladder and cutting away pieces of the nets as souvenirs.

Bryant averaged 31 points, 12 rebounds, 6.5 assists, 4 steals, and 3.8 blocks per game in taking Merion to an impressive 31-3 record and the school's first state title in 50 years. He gained national distinction and was named the Naismith and the Gatorade High School Player of the Year and earned a spot on an all-star team sponsored by McDonald's. He also earned the attention of college and pro scouts. A huge decision loomed in Kobe Bryant's future.

Chapter 2

Kobe the Professional

Most graduates from high school face the decision of whether to go to college, and if so, which university to attend. Bryant grew up with a deep love of books and the academic world, but he was enticed by the prospect of being one of a few players who would bypass college and go directly to the professional basketball ranks. In the end, Bryant followed his dream.

To the NBA

All the top college coaches and programs wanted Bryant, including two of the most respected—Mike Krzyzewski at Duke University and the University of North Carolina's Dean Smith. The beautiful campuses, with their impressive buildings and solid academic reputations, held great appeal, and Bryant knew that only a handful of athletes had successfully made the arduous transition from high school basketball to professional competition. He understood that every one of those players had been a muscular athlete who relied on a more physical game than the flashy one Bryant employed, and he wondered if he could handle the more physically taxing regimen required by the long NBA season and by competing against bigger opponents. If he selected the NBA, he would spend much time on the bench while he learned the intricacies of NBA play, while in college he would be a starter from the first day.

La Salle University basketball coach Phil Martelli hoped Bryant would remain in the Philadelphia area and attend his school, but he doubted he would have the chance to coach the star. He said, "Kobe is a genius. He's like one of those kids who graduates from college at the age of thirteen." Martelli, who often watched Bryant work out and shoot baskets at the La Salle gym, was most impressed with Bryant's determination to succeed. The coach even told his players that if they wanted to improve their games, "check out his work ethic."[25]

On April 29, 1996, before a packed gymnasium at Lower Merion High School and an array of local and national reporters in attendance, Bryant announced that he would head directly to the NBA. "Playing in the NBA has been my dream since I was three,"[26] he told the excited crowd. He explained

On April 29, 1996, before a packed gymnasium at Lower Merion High School and an array of local and national reporters in attendance, Kobe announced that he would head directly to the NBA.

that it was time for him to embark on that dream. Two weeks later, Bryant announced a $10 million deal to market a Kobe Bryant basketball shoe with Adidas and signed with one of the most respected talent agencies in the country, the William Morris Agency.

Some people condemned Bryant's parents for allowing their son to abandon college. Many wondered how an eighteen-year-old would handle the fast-paced lifestyle enjoyed by athletes five and ten years his senior. Jon Jennings, the director of basketball development for the Boston Celtics, called it "a total mistake. Kevin Garnett was the best high school player I ever saw, and I wouldn't have advised him to jump to the NBA. And Kobe is no Kevin Garnett."[27]

Others answered that many high school graduates opt out of college to follow other pursuits, and that the strong support provided by his family would see him through any obstacles. Pamela Bryant remarked that they were prepared to support Kobe's dream no matter what it was, and Joe explained that, rather than being their choice as some detractors stated, Kobe had examined all the factors and made his own decision. "This was Kobe's dream, so it's his decision."[28]

A Laker

Before the draft occurs, NBA teams screen prospective athletes to determine which player they might draft. They normally rely on lengthy interviews, a brief practice session on the court, and studying game tapes. For much of May and June, Bryant participated in a series of grueling tryouts for various NBA teams, each time receiving high marks.

Jerry West, general manager for the Los Angeles Lakers and a Hall of Fame NBA guard from the 1960s, put Bryant through an especially rigorous scrimmage, tossing him into one-on-one contests against former Lakers players and against one of the top college prospects. Bryant so impressed West that the executive started figuring out how to grab Bryant in the draft. As his team had compiled a good record the year before, they would not select until twenty-six other teams had made their choices, and West figured Bryant would be gone by then. If he were to obtain Bryant, West would have to arrange a trade with another team to move up in the draft order.

West pulled off his surprise on draft day, June 16. On the thirteenth pick, the Charlotte Hornets, who had never talked to Bryant or asked him to fly in for a workout, selected the Pennsylvania star. On the sly, West and the Hornets had worked out a deal. Charlotte wanted an experienced big man to play center or forward, and West wanted to draft Bryant as well as rid himself of a veteran player so he could take the money he might have paid that athlete and give it to free agent and All-Star center Shaquille O'Neal of the Orlando Magic. For Charlotte's selection in the draft, West agreed to trade his 7-foot-1-inch center (216cm), Vlade Divac.

In rapid order, Bryant became a Hornet, and soon afterward a Laker. The moment became a highlight for a young man who had posters of great Lakers players adorning his room and who had always imagined playing for his favorite team. "I'm going out there to answer a challenge that I put to myself since the ninth grade,"[29] said an excited Bryant to assembled reporters.

To those who claimed he erred in abandoning college, Bryant said he would work twice as hard to prove them wrong, and added that he simply could not pass up a chance to play professional ball. "When I'm forty, if I sit back and say, 'Man, I went to the NBA, I gave it my all, and I failed,' it happens," Bryant said. "But I couldn't accept not going to the NBA and giving it my all. I can't accept that."[30]

On July 12, the Lakers introduced their new acquisition to the Los Angeles media. Bryant said all the right things, praising the team and its past stars. "I'm very excited to be here. It's a dream come true to play in the NBA and to come to a team like L.A. that had a great history, great players like Magic Johnson and Kareem Abdul-Jabbar. It was a team I looked up to when I was growing up, and now here I am playing pickup basketball with Magic Johnson at UCLA."[31]

A Huge Trade

The trade between the Los Angeles Lakers and the Charlotte Hornets, arranged by Jerry West, benefited both teams. The Hornets were badly in need of a proven player rather than an untested college or high school athlete. As Bob Bass, the Hornets' executive vice president of basketball operations, said:

> When you look back at it, when we made that trade, here was a 17-year-old kid who had played in high school. Twelve other teams passed on him. We made a decision to win now and not later. We had Dave Cowens as our first-year coach, and I wanted to give him a chance to win. I knew if we got [Vlade] Divac in here, we'd win. I didn't feel the same about Bryant. Without Divac, I thought we might have won 25 games.

The move worked, as the Hornets, with Divac anchoring their team, won fifty-four games, a then franchise record.

Quoted in John Delong. "Lakers' Trade for Bryant Has Been Misconstrued." *Winston-Salem (NC) Journal*, June 18, 2008. www2.journalnow.com/sports/2008/jun/18/lakers-trade-for-bryant-has-been-misconstrued-ar-113126.

The trade between Los Angeles and Charlotte for Kobe, arranged by Jerry West, benefited both teams.

Jerry West announced the team's intention to bring the player along slowly. Rather than start, Bryant would be brought in a few minutes at a time and only enjoy increased time when he had better learned the system and had proved he deserved to play more. West added, though, that within six years Bryant would be one of the game's top attractions.

When questioned about the adjustments he would have to make—he was, after all, a recent high school graduate about to become immersed in a man's world—Bryant vowed not to let the money and glamorous Hollywood lifestyle affect him. He preferred video games and movies at home to glittering nightclubs and adoring females, and he knew that he had to remain focused on basketball. "The only thing I want to do right now in L.A. is play and win a championship,"[32] Bryant said. To help him through the adjustment period, Bryant's parents and sisters moved to Los Angeles and lived in an expansive mansion he purchased in Pacific Palisades, a wealthy suburb of Los Angeles.

After averaging 25 points a game for a Lakers team in a summer league, Bryant suffered a setback in early September when he broke his wrist trying to dunk. The injury caused him to miss part of the team's training camp, but he returned on October 16 to score 10 points in his first professional exhibition game. Twelve days later, another injury forced him to miss more action, making some wonder if Bryant was too small to play with the bigger NBA stars.

Bryant compensated for his lack of muscle by studying game film more intently than ever. He thought that if he could not overpower opponents, he could discover their weaknesses and attack those. He knew he was lighter than most kids his age and he wanted to develop an edge to compensate for his size.

For instance, Bryant spent hours studying Dallas Maverick Jimmy Jackson before their upcoming exhibition game. By the time the contest arrived, Bryant knew what moves the player favored, and the first time he guarded Jackson, Bryant swiped the ball from the surprised veteran. "It was only a preseason game, but I prepared for it like it was the state championship,"[33] Bryant recalled.

Protective Parents

Kobe Bryant enjoyed living in a close family, one in which the parents interacted with their children and took an active interest in what they were doing. That role even included choosing which movies their son watched. "My wife and I used to prescreen movies before we'd let the kids see them," said Joe Bryant. "We used to push the kids under the seat when the actors would start kissing." Kobe did not see *The Godfather*, which became his favorite movie, until his parents thought he was mature enough to handle the violence. When he finally did view the film, he thought of his own family. "It reminds me of my family," Kobe said. "Not because of the violence, but because of the way they all pulled for each other no matter what."

Quoted in Ian Thomsen. "Showtime!." *Sports Illustrated*, April 27, 1998. http://sports illustrated.cnn.com/vault/article/magazine/MAG1012689/index.htm.

Period of Adjustment

Like most rookies, Bryant faced a situation he had never encountered before. Instead of being the star player on a team of supporting characters, as had been true in high school, he was now cast in a supporting role with and against athletes every bit as skilled as he was. Until he learned the game's nuances, he could barely count on leaving the bench. In the first eleven games of the regular season, Bryant struggled to get off a decent shot and turned the ball over more frequently than he ever had. According to his coach and a few team players, he was trying to force something to happen when he needed to relax, learn the professional game, and allow things to unfold.

He had to earn his minutes on the court, especially with a coach who remained skeptical over handling a youth only months removed from high school. "Here's this kid in a man's game and he's not ready," fretted coach Del Harris. "He should be on another team that isn't expected to win right now."[34]

Bryant made things worse by not going to his veteran team-mates and asking for advice, a slight that some did not forget. "It was clear that Kobe just didn't understand the way things work on a team," explained one former Laker. "He came in wanting to shine from the very beginning. He didn't go to the older guys like most younger guys usually do. They wait and learn from everyone else."[35]

Bryant was named to the Rookie Team as part of the All-Star weekend festivities. Against the league's top first-year players, Bryant scored a game-high 31 points, a scoring record for a rookie, and topped that by capturing the slam dunk contest.

No one could deny his potential though. In a victory against the Phoenix Suns, Bryant hit four of six 3-point shots and scored 16 points, and he played well enough as the season unfolded that the league named him to the rookie team as part of the All-Star weekend festivities. Against the league's top first-year players, Bryant scored a game-high 31 points, a scoring record for a rookie, and topped that by capturing the slam dunk contest.

Bryant admitted that being a part of a team with men eight to twelve years older was more difficult than he had imagined. Many teammates came from different backgrounds than the more sheltered Bryant, who had spent most of his formative years in Italy and in a wealthy Philadelphia suburb. The teen-

Kobe Wants the Ball

Bryant never shied from taking the final shot. He earned a reputation in high school for bringing his team through in tough predicaments, and when he joined the NBA, he expected to do the same. He quickly learned, however, that what worked in high school did not necessarily work in professional games.

He made certain to let his coach know how he felt. "He said, 'Coach, if you just give me the ball and clear out, I can beat anybody in this league,'" said Del Harris. When that approach failed to work, Bryant returned with another attempt. Harris recalled, "Then he'd say, 'Coach, I can post up [drive to the basket against] anybody who's guarding me. If you just get me in there and clear it out, I can post up anybody.'" Though impressed that his rookie player wanted the ball, Harris kept turning him down. "I said, 'Kobe, I know you can, but right now you can't do it at a high enough rate for the team we have, and I'm not going to tell Shaq [O'Neal] to get out of the way so you can do this.' Kobe didn't like it. He understood it, but in his heart he didn't accept it."

Quoted in Chris Ballard. "Kobe's Well-Honed Killer Instinct." *Sports Illustrated*, May 28, 2008. http://sportsillustrated.cnn.com/vault/article/web/COM1138889/index.htm.

ager found it hard to chat with men approaching thirty, and as a result he kept more to himself. Two players, Eddie Jones and Byron Scott, took time to sit down with Bryant and help him manage the transition, but he still seemed to have trouble bonding with his teammates.

He kept to himself in the locker room and sat alone in the back of the airplane while teammates played cards. Instead of joining other players after the game for a visit to a nightclub or restaurant, Bryant retreated to his hotel room or home to watch videos. "He's never really been a guy to hang out, not even in high school," said one of Bryant's friends in the NBA, Cuttino Mobley, who knew Bryant in Philadelphia. "He's a private dude and I think many guys just didn't understand that. And when you add that he wasn't from the inner city, like most of us, they really didn't understand him. And what you don't understand, you don't like."[36]

He clashed with the team's star and captain, Shaquille O'Neal, who felt the rookie forgot to pay him the respect due a man who had attained so much in the game. Before Bryant was out of high school, O'Neal had been an NBA All-Star four times, had led the league in scoring once, and had been named the 1993 NBA Rookie of the Year. Instead of seeking advice from O'Neal or praising the center, Bryant seemed to avoid him. Like O'Neal, Bryant loved the limelight, and Lakers fans adored the flashy rookie, who would never easily accept being placed in a secondary role to any other player. "Kobe didn't care that Shaq was the veteran with the experience," said a Lakers staff member. "He didn't want to listen or defer, and he knew he didn't have to because the fans were on his side. For whatever reason, fans loved Kobe from the moment he hit town."[37]

"I think some of the guys thought he held himself above everyone else," added Billy Hunter, president of the NBA Players Association. "They had issues with him because of that attitude." Even his friend Cuttino Mobley said that Bryant displayed too much arrogance. "We're all arrogant, but Kobe just had more confidence in his ability."[38]

The season changed for the Lakers after the All-Star break. Due to injuries to starting players, Harris had to rely on his bench to provide scoring punch. In an April game against the Golden State Warriors, Bryant scored a game-high 24 points to lift the Lakers into a first-place tie. Though the team did not remain in first place, their 56-26 regular season record was their best in seven years and earned the Lakers a spot in the playoffs. For the season, Bryant averaged 7.6 points per game and showed enough talent that onlookers predicted he would soon anchor the team's offense.

Bryant saw little action in a first-round series against the Portland Trail Blazers, which the Lakers won 3-1. He left the bench more frequently against the Utah Jazz in the Western Conference semifinal match, and while he notched 19 points in one contest, he suffered his worst moment on the court in the loss that ended their playoff run. With the game tied and time about to expire, Bryant lofted a potential game-winning shot from 14 feet (4.27m) out that embarrassingly ended up an air ball—it hit neither the basket nor the net. As if that were not bad enough, in overtime Bryant launched three shots that could have helped his team to victory, but each one hit nothing but air. In a clutch situation, Bryant, who prided himself on his ability to produce when it most mattered, had come up pitifully short.

While even Shaquille O'Neal told reporters that he was impressed with the rookie's willingness to be either goat or hero and take the pressure-laden shots, Bryant was mortified. "They already hate me," Bryant said to Jocelyn Ebron about his teammates. "Now they just hate me more."[39]

The 1997–1998 Season

Bryant wasted no time trying to correct his failure to make those four shots. The next morning, he took hundreds of jump shots at a nearby gym, concentrating on the spot on the floor from which he had missed the crucial attempts. He hired a personal trainer to create a rigorous program that included running sprints six days a week, followed by weight training and more hours on the court. In a summer professional league, he followed his coach's advice to work on team play and on patience. His coaches believed that he had been more interested

The NBA Playoff System

The NBA playoff system has experienced many changes since its inception in 1947, mainly due to league expansion. The thirty-team league is currently divided into the Eastern and the Western Conferences, each containing three divisions of five teams each. The three division winners in each conference, plus the five teams with the next-best records, enter the playoffs.

The playoffs begin in two brackets, one for the eight playoff teams of the Eastern Conference and one for the eight playoff teams of the Western Conference. The initial round, the first of four best-of-seven series, narrows the field to four teams apiece in the two conferences. Those victors enter the second round, called the conference semifinals. The winners of the second round—two in each conference—advance to the conference finals. The two teams that emerge on top are designated the conference champions, and those teams square off in the ultimate series, the last best-of-seven contest, to determine the NBA Finals champion.

in making impressive moves on the court and taking a potentially game-winning basket than involving his teammates, and that he too readily tried to make something happen rather than waiting for an opening to develop for an easy shot or quick pass to someone else. He labored up to eight hours a day to become a better shooter and a stronger athlete—and he gained 10 pounds (4.5kg) that summer.

Magic Johnson, Bryant's childhood hero, was at the gym that first day after the playoffs and watched Bryant sweat and labor at a time when most of his Lakers teammates took time off for a vacation. "That was just like me," said Johnson. "I loved seeing that from him. That's how I reacted, too. This is where he needs to be."[40]

Most Lakers looked optimistically toward the start of the 1997–1998 season. O'Neal was only twenty-five and in the

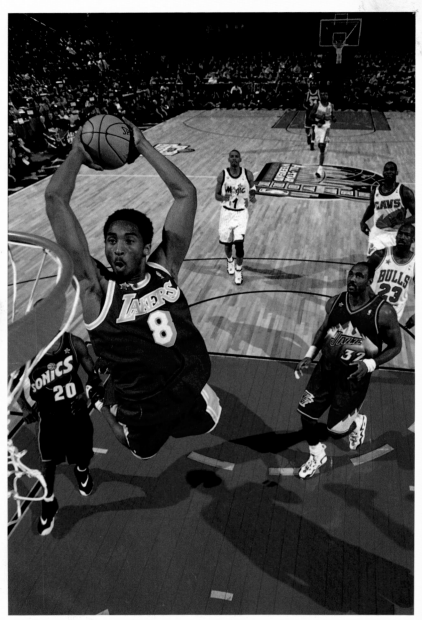

People began comparing Bryant with Michael Jordan, the famed Chicago Bulls star, and fans voted him to start in the NBA All-Star Game, a feat making Bryant the youngest starter in All-Star history.

prime of his career, and he played with a solid supporting cast of younger teammates, including Nick Van Exel, Eddie Jones, and the nineteen-year-old Bryant. When the quartet led the team to wins in its first eleven games, thoughts of a possible championship run increased.

Those hopes took a hard blow when O'Neal suffered an abdominal injury and missed twenty games. In his absence, however, Bryant and the other Lakers stepped up, focused on playing together, and won thirteen of the twenty contests. Observers sensed a different Bryant than the one from the previous season, one more willing to involve his teammates in the action. "If you didn't know how old he is," said Vlade Divac, the man traded so the Lakers could acquire Bryant, "it would be normal. But he's a nineteen-year-old kid playing like a thirty-year-old."[41]

His outstanding play gained praise on and off the court. Other players began comparing Bryant with Michael Jordan, the famed Chicago Bulls star, and fans voted him to start in the NBA All-Star Game, a feat making Bryant the youngest starter in All-Star history.

Though some thought Bryant had changed—he had even invited his teammates to his nineteenth birthday party shortly before the season—Bryant's tendency to take over games reappeared before long. Teammates claimed he hogged the ball, and during one practice session, Bryant and O'Neal had to be separated after O'Neal smacked Bryant to the floor. Western Conference coach George Karl even benched him in the fourth quarter of the All-Star Game when some of the other players complained about Bryant's selfish play.

Harris pledged to correct this flaw in his young athlete. While most basketball players go to college, where they are involved in a team system, Bryant had never had that experience. Harris concluded that the only way to teach Bryant this lesson was to cut back on his playing time until he was ready to be more of a team player than an individual.

The turmoil surrounding Bryant affected his play. He hated having his playing time reduced, and opposing teams had begun to alter their defenses by assigning two men to guard Bryant. In the final two months of the season, however, all the pieces fell into place. Behind a torrid scoring streak from O'Neal, including a 50-point showing in a win over New Jersey, and a more involved Bryant, the Lakers won twenty-two of their final twenty-five games to compile a 61-21 record and capture the Pacific Division title.

Hopes for a championship soared. The Lakers knocked off Portland 3-1, with Bryant taking a supporting role. When they defeated the Seattle SuperSonics 4-1 in the second round, a championship seemed closer.

Featuring stars Karl Malone and John Stockton, however, the Utah Jazz swept the Lakers in four games to end their title hopes. Bryant headed to another off-season, this time disappointed with his own play and with the team's performance. Bryant was intent on becoming a more mature player the next year.

Growing Pains

The 1998–1999 season unraveled almost before it began, as the Lakers and the NBA endured a series of crucial changes. A contract dispute between team owners and the players' union caused a lockout that pushed back the start of the season three months. When the season finally started, the Lakers were a far different team than before. Eleven games after the season finally started in January, the Lakers fired Del Harris and replaced him with former Laker Kurt Rambis. The team acquired Dennis Rodman, a rebounding machine whose off-court antics kept him in the headlines, and traded Eddie Jones and Elden Campbell for Glen Rice and J.R. Reid. The Lakers hoped the changes would create a unit that played together and prod veteran members to increase their effort.

Discontented Lakers players vented their anger at Bryant, again raising the charge that he hogged the ball. Bryant and O'Neal argued in practice, with O'Neal claiming Bryant wanted to steal the spotlight from him and Bryant countering that O'Neal failed to work as hard as he should. O'Neal made no attempt to hide from reporters his displeasure that Los Angeles fans seemed to favor the teenager over him, and again thought that Bryant should show more respect for him.

Magic Johnson talked to both stars. He tried to persuade Bryant to be friendlier off the court and join his teammates in various activities, and he told O'Neal that he had only won his championships because he had teamed with another star athlete, Kareem Abdul-Jabbar. Bryant, who had never felt comfortable with Los Angeles nightclubs and parties, said he would try to improve but promised nothing, while O'Neal brushed aside advice from Johnson concerning his feud with Bryant.

The turmoil bothered Bryant. He thought he was doing what was best for the team and only took shots to help them win games, not to gain personal glory. His high school teams had always relied on him to come through for them, and he thought it would be the same in the NBA. He had not counted on the fact that the NBA contained other players just like him, men who also wanted the chance to win games.

"There are times when I go home and think the Lord has given me a lot to deal with," said Bryant. "But I always come to the conclusion that he would never put more of a burden on a person's shoulders than they are ready to bear." When a reporter asked Bryant if he was a happy teenager, he answered, "I guess, maybe. Not really. I really don't believe in happiness."[42]

Lakers general manager Jerry West wondered if the athlete he drafted might have been better off emotionally and physically by attending college first. He told a reporter at that time that a more mature Bryant would have been able to better handle, or even avoid, the controversy that seemed to follow him.

A Rocky Playoff

The Lakers again gained a spot in the playoffs with a 31-19 record, with O'Neal a dominant force underneath the basket and Bryant averaging almost 20 points. Before the first round, the team held a players-only meeting to discuss their differences and smooth over hurt feelings. Many agreed that maybe they had forgotten just how young Bryant still was. "We look at all the attention and hype he gets and think he shouldn't be making all those mistakes," said Lakers forward Rick Fox. "But we forget he's just a kid. We just sort of left him hanging this season, an island by himself, and that's going to stop. He wants to win as much as anyone else, and he deserves our support."[43]

When the Lakers swept the Houston Rockets in the first round, matters seemed settled. Bryant avoided the fatal errors he had been making by trying to do too much and, in the process, either turning over the ball or throwing up an ill-advised shot. However, the San Antonio Spurs sent the Lakers home to an early summer vacation by containing O'Neal and Bryant on the way to sweeping the four-game series.

Though Bryant posted a subpar performance in the playoffs, he had shown enough in his first three seasons to earn a six-year extension to his contract worth $70 million. Bryant enjoyed financial stability, but he lacked the two things he most wanted—respect from NBA players and NBA championships.

Chapter 3

A Championship Team

Kobe Bryant had now put together three solid years in the NBA, but like every athlete to make it to the professional ranks, he coveted a championship title. Bryant was familiar with enough basketball history to know that many great performers never wore a championship ring. They may have gained individual honors, scoring titles, and All-Star accolades, but they could not claim they were champions. Bryant intended to avoid being placed in that undesirable category.

A New Coach

He found help in a new coach. During the summer of 1999, the Lakers hired former Chicago Bulls head coach Phil Jackson to take over the reins. Jackson brought a stellar reputation with him, as he had won six championships coaching Michael Jordan and the Bulls in the 1990s. If anyone could gain the respect of Bryant and O'Neal, the two Lakers stars who had yet to find a way to mesh their games, it would be Jackson.

Jackson relied on what he called the triangle offense to propel his team, a method that offered more creativity and ball movement for players. Rather than depending on a rigid offense that dictated where each man should be, Jackson's tactics allowed the team to react to what the opposing defense did. The new coach, a deeply intellectual man who asked his players to read biographies and philosophy in preparation for the season, thought his system would be perfect for Bryant and O'Neal, as it gave them the chance to either shoot or pass depending on the situation. Jackson also counted on the fact that both players had yet to win a championship to work in his favor. O'Neal and Bryant wanted an NBA title; Jackson had coached the Bulls to six.

Bryant was so elated with the hire that on the day Jackson was introduced as head coach, Bryant made a surprise visit to the coach's hotel room to let the coach know how excited he was and that he would one day like to be team captain, a spot held by O'Neal. Jackson reminded Bryant that he could hardly be team captain if none of the players were willing to follow him and asked that he think more of the team than himself.

Jackson wasted little time asserting his authority on the team. He informed the Lakers, who had gained a reputation for throwing wild parties after games, that the good times were over. From now on, basketball was to be a serious business for all, one that asked complete concentration. "Phil came in here and told this team to grow up and stop being little boys," said newcomer John Salley, himself the holder of championship rings from his days with the Detroit Pistons. "Be men and play the game the way it's supposed to be played. It's that simple."[44]

Jackson then addressed the issue on everyone's mind—the Bryant-O'Neal split. He stated that from that point on, he as coach was the leader of the Lakers and everyone else occupied a supporting role. He would plan the offensive and defensive tactics, he would prepare the team, and they would take his ideas and execute them on the court. Jackson challenged both Bryant and O'Neal to subordinate personal interests to team victory.

Both players agreed to heed their coach's wishes. O'Neal, who grew up in a military family, told reporters he needed a take-charge coach like Jackson. "I needed to be challenged," said O'Neal. "Phil immediately told me what was wrong with my game and what to do to change it. That's what I always had at home. I always had the complete game, but other coaches told me to just shoot, shoot and shoot so I took the shot when I got it. Now with Phil's system it allows me to pass, block, dunk—all those things that get me on the highlight reel on ESPN."[45]

During the summer of 1999 the Lakers hired former Chicago Bulls head coach, Phil Jackson. If anyone could gain the respect of Bryant and O'Neal, the two Lakers stars who had yet to find a way to mesh their games, it would be him.

Jackson seemed a genius when the Lakers swept to the top in the first months of the season, taking twenty-five of the first thirty games. Bryant's speed and ball-handling talent was a perfect match for the new offense, as fans began seeing a new side to the young star who passed to the open man and dribbled around and through defenders. He and O'Neal played as a duo, with one man leading the way to victory one night and the other the next. O'Neal earned Player of the Month in three different months, and Bryant became the youngest player ever to receive All-Defensive honors, a tribute to his emphasis on defense and team play. By season's end, the Lakers had captured the Pacific Division title with a 67-15 record and home court advantage throughout the playoffs.

A Championship Ring

The Lakers worked their way into the NBA Finals with series wins over the Sacramento Kings, Phoenix Suns, and Portland Trail Blazers. The series against the Trail Blazers was a grueling seven-game bloodbath that required the Lakers to overcome a 13-point deficit in the fourth quarter of the deciding game. With the victory, Bryant was about to play in his first NBA Finals, but his dream of holding a championship trophy faced one stern obstacle—the Indiana Pacers and their coach, Hall of Fame basketball star Larry Bird.

O'Neal dominated Game 1, a Lakers win in which he scored 43 points and snared 19 rebounds. The Lakers won Game 2 as well, but in the process lost Bryant to a badly sprained ankle. Team doctors could not predict whether Bryant could be back before the end of the series, but anyone who knew Bryant stated that the star would get back on the court as soon as possible.

Phil Jackson knew the Pacers would come out hard in Game 4, because if they won that contest, the series would be knotted at two games apiece and everything would be up for grabs. If the Lakers triumphed, on the other hand, the series would be 3-1 in their favor. The Pacers marched to a 100-91 win in Game 3 when, with Bryant sitting on the bench and unable to participate, they double-teamed O'Neal every time he handled the ball. At this point, all seemed to depend on whether Bryant's ankle would allow him to play.

Though limping from the ankle injury, Bryant returned to the court for Game 4. The lead seesawed for most of the game, which wound up tied in regulation when the Pacers' Sam Perkins made a 3-point shot as time expired, sending the game into overtime. With the score tied at 104, O'Neal fouled out. As O'Neal headed to the bench, Bryant walked over to his teammate and said, "I got you."[46] In other words, Bryant was going to pick up the slack.

Jackson sensed that, with the game on the line, now was the time to hand matters over to Bryant. Despite being hobbled with the bad ankle, Bryant, who had missed clutch playoff shots earlier in his career, notched 8 points in overtime to take the Lakers to a 120-118 win. Larry Bird, who enjoyed a reputation as one of the game's all-time great clutch shooters, said afterward that he knew the Lakers were going to get the ball to Bryant, but he simply could not devise a strategy to stop the player from scoring. Bryant scored 26 points in Game 4, including two pressure-packed free throws in the final six seconds. "This is the

Coach Jackson sensed that, with the game on the line, it was time to hand matters over to Bryant. Despite an ankle injury Kobe was able to take charge on the court and took his team to a 120-118 win.

Michael Jackson

Kobe Bryant freely admitted that Lakers coach Phil Jackson and his insistence on team play had much to do with his gaining his first NBA title. Bryant also admitted he learned from others, some of whom never set foot on a basketball court. As he explained, help in how to prepare for games once came from the music industry, when singer Michael Jackson called Bryant one day and invited him for a visit. Bryant explained:

> We could always talk about how he prepared to make his music, how he prepared for concerts. He would teach me what he did. How to make a "Thriller" album, a "Bad" album. All the details that went into it. It was all the validation that I needed—to know that I had to focus on my craft and never waver. Because what he did—and how he did it—was psychotic. He helped me get to a level where I was able to win three titles playing with Shaq (Shaquille O'Neal) because of my preparation, my study.

> It's not from [Michael] Jordan. It's not from other athletes. It's from Michael Jackson.

Quoted in Terry Foster. "King of Pop Proved a Mentor to Kobe Bryant." *Detroit News*, November 25, 2010. http://detnews.com/article/20101125/OPINION03/11250320/1127/sports/King-of-Pop-proved-a-mentor-to-Kobe-Bryant.

After meeting and talking to pop star Michael Jackson, Bryant knew he had to focus on his craft and never waver. Jackson helped him get to a level where he was able to win three titles playing with Shaq because of his preparation and his study.

game I've been dreaming about, to be honest with you," Bryant said after the game. "I dream about it every day."[47]

Other players agreed that, with O'Neal out of the game, Bryant took matters into his own hands. "I was watching what he did tonight and I was thinking about those old NBA classic films, Magic and Kareem and others just taking over games in the finals," teammate Derek Fisher said. "Tonight, he took a chapter right out of their book."[48]

John Salley claimed that every Laker on the court knew to get out of Bryant's way. He had that look in his eyes, and they knew he would somehow bring them to victory. "Kobe smelled it, and he lifted us,"[49] Jackson said.

Now up 3-1, the Lakers had the Pacers' backs to the wall. Determined not to lose the championship on their home court, the Pacers took Game 5, 120-87, sending the series back to Los Angeles. Though trailing for much of the game, the Lakers went on a 15-6 run in the fourth quarter with solid shooting from Bryant and rebounding from O'Neal to take the lead. When the Pacers came back to tie it with five minutes remaining, Bryant once again took charge and took his team to a 116-111 win. The dream of possessing an NBA championship was Bryant's at last.

Though in his jubilation he could not imagine it, more were to follow. At the same time, the first hints of trouble in his life surfaced.

Lesson Learned?

Bryant had compiled such an impressive record throughout his career because, like most top-flight athletes, he kept adding new objectives. When he achieved one—in this case, an NBA title—he turned to others. When he told people that he now wanted a second consecutive championship and, along with it, the league's Most Valuable Player (MVP) Award, he set his sights on two achievements—a team goal and a personal one.

He kept teammates after practice so he could try out new moves, and he so speedily became adept that he amazed players. His high school coach, Gregg Downer, claimed it was this intense focus on being great that made Bryant both a star and created some of his problems. "I think Kobe's actually a little bit embarrassed by his love of basketball," said Downer. "People called him a loner, but it's just that basketball is all he wants to focus on. I think he's part of a dying breed that loves the game that way."[50]

He loved the game, but sometimes forgot that the game depended upon team play. Teammates raised eyebrows when Bryant told them before the season that now that he had a championship ring, he wanted a scoring title and an MVP trophy. They told their coach they were concerned that Bryant would again be more focused on his personal goals rather than being a good team player. Their concerns increased when the team stumbled to a slow start, losing sixteen of the first forty-seven games, one more than in the transpose season. Bryant amassed points along the way and delighted crowds with spins and jumps, but left teammates standing alone with open shots. At the same time, O'Neal started the season overweight and out of shape.

Conditions soured to such an extent that Jackson stepped in. The intellectual Bryant admired his coach's dedication to the game and his ability to thoroughly analyze basketball, and he loved Jackson's triangle offense because it challenged players to think constantly about the game, much as if they were involved in a chess match with their opponent. Now, though, the coach took Bryant aside and cautioned him that if he could not learn to work better with O'Neal and his teammates, Bryant would be traded.

"Some players understand early on that everyone makes sacrifices for the team," said veteran forward Robert Horry, who had won two championships with the Houston Rockets before joining the Lakers. "Some take forever to get it. And some just have to relearn it every year."[51]

A March ankle injury that sent Bryant to the bench caused him to reassess his role and confirmed Jackson's advice. Rather than struggle in Bryant's absence, the Lakers began playing better basketball. As he watched the team roll up a string of victories, Bryant saw what a team could do if they acted as a unit rather than as individuals. He started to see the game differently and to realize how much better the Lakers would be if he became an integral part of the team. When he returned, Bryant set aside individual glory for team accomplishment, and fellow players began seeing Bryant pass the ball and occupy a supporting role.

"When you sit on the bench, you see the game in different ways," explains Bryant. "You make the adjustments you have to make to win. It should be no surprise that, despite the rocky stuff, we got it together."[52] The team finished the regular season by winning the final eight games and again gained a Pacific Division title. Reflective of Bryant's team approach, the Lakers star earned a berth on the All-NBA Second Team, while teammate O'Neal enjoyed a spot on the First Team. The All-NBA Team is an honor given by the league at the end of the year to recognize quality play throughout the entire season

They continued their stellar play in the playoffs. Bryant's unselfish style meshed perfectly with the rest of the team, and the Lakers registered an astonishing 15-1 record to take their second straight NBA crown. An impressed O'Neal even called Bryant the best player in the league.

He Gains a Wife, but Loses a Family

In November 1999, the twenty-one-year-old Bryant met sixteen-year-old Vanessa Laine, a high school sophomore, while she danced in a music video being made by Bryant's rapper friend, Snoop Dogg. Despite the difference in ages, the two clicked immediately, and soon, to the astonishment of students and teachers, Bryant began dropping Laine off at Marina High School in Huntington Beach in the mornings. The unusual match made school authorities uncomfortable, and they eventually asked Bryant to stop bringing her to school and attending school events.

Bryant's family reacted even more vehemently. They warned their son that he had little in common with the high school student, who to Bryant's parents appeared to want nothing more than their son's money and fame. They were also uncomfortable that Laine was not African American, and they begged Bryant

When Laine was a senior, Bryant proposed with a seven-carat diamond engagement ring. His parents bitterly objected, and when their opposition failed to influence Bryant, they vowed not to attend the wedding.

to avoid rushing to the altar. When the relationship heated up, Phil Jackson advised Bryant to wait a few years until Laine was older and Bryant could be certain that she was the one for him.

"We all knew he got so attached to her because he needed a friend, someone to hang out with," explained a fellow Laker. "I'm not sure if it was love, or he was just happy that someone accepted him with no complaints. He didn't understand that she was a kid and she was in awe of him."[53]

Bryant was in no mood to listen to advice. When Laine was a senior, Bryant proposed with a seven-carat diamond engagement ring. His parents bitterly objected, and when their opposition failed to influence Bryant, they vowed not to attend the wedding. On April 18, 2001, Bryant married Laine in a small ceremony witnessed by neither Bryant's family nor his teammates. Shortly afterward, when Bryant sold the mansion he and his family had lived in, Joe and Pamela Bryant returned to Philadelphia.

Bryant did not speak to his family until September 11, 2001, the day two airplanes crashed into New York City's World Trade Center towers. His mother subsequently invited Bryant and his wife for the Christmas holidays, but Bryant declined when his wife objected. The next February, the pair traveled to Philadelphia for the All-Star Game, during which Lower Merion High School retired Bryant's jersey. Bryant's parents attended but sat on the opposite side of the court from their son's wife.

The 2001–2002 Season

Matters on the court were not as tumultuous. Seeking a third consecutive NBA crown, the Lakers won sixteen of their first seventeen games and had compiled a 33-13 record by the midseason break. With O'Neal and Bryant finishing in the top six leaders in scoring, the team finished the season with a 58-24 record, second best in the league.

The Lakers would play in another playoff, the time of the season Bryant most loved because of the increased pressure to win. The Lakers swept Portland in three games to advance to the second round, where they defeated San Antonio, four games to one. The Bryant trademark of scoring game-winning baskets again appeared, as he made two 3-pointers to tie one game before scoring the game-winning points in another of the contests.

"I love playing in pressure-type situations," Bryant said after the game. "I've grown into this role, to deliver when the game is on the line." He added that when the players left the huddle

To Be the Best

Kobe Bryant is both cursed and blessed by his intense desire to be the best. That determination drives him to the success he has enjoyed, but it has also offended some, who claim he is driven more by personal acclaim than team glory. He even hates to lose in pickup games or practice. Brian Shaw, Bryant's teammate for four years, explained:

> If you scored on him in practice or did something to embarrass him, he would just keep on challenging you and challenging you until you stayed after and played him so he could put his will on you and dominate you. . . . He'd stand in our way and say, "Nah, nah, we're gonna play. I want you to do that [move] again." ... And you might be tired and say, "Nah, I did it in practice." But he was just relentless and persistent until finally you'd go play, and he'd go at you.

Quoted in Chris Ballard. "Kobe's Well-Honed Killer Instinct." *Sports Illustrated*, May 28, 2008. http://sportsillustrated.cnn.com/vault/article/web/COM1138889/index.htm.

before the final shot, one of his teammates told him to seal the win. Bryant answered that he would. "This is what I live for,"[54] he confidently replied.

The Lakers next engaged in a hard-fought series with the Sacramento Kings, the team that had the best record in the league and was expected to pose a difficult obstacle. After splitting the first six games, the Kings forced a deciding game seven against the Lakers. The Lakers won the final game in overtime, with Bryant feeding baskets to open teammates and tossing in clutch shots and O'Neal dominating in the middle. At twenty-three, Bryant became the youngest player in NBA history to own three conference championships.

The New Jersey Nets posed little problem in the finals, which the Lakers won in four games. O'Neal gained Most Valuable Player honors for the third consecutive time, but Bryant displayed a willingness to be a team player by accepting Jackson's tactics and playing second fiddle to O'Neal during the first three quarters, and then taking the lead role in the fourth quarters when opponents began focusing on O'Neal. He scored 12 points in the fourth quarter of Game 3 and 11 in Game 4 to assure both wins. Bryant averaged almost 27 points a game for the series, shooting an astonishing 63 percent in the fourth quarters, but more importantly, added 6 rebounds and 5 assists.

"We rely on Kobe's maturity, leadership and ability to take over a game when he has to and knowing when that time is," said Phil Jackson. "Together, he and Shaquille make quite a pair."[55]

In being named to the All-NBA First Team, Bryant showed that he had improved his team play enough that other people around the league had taken notice. In many ways, Bryant grew as an all-around athlete and team player. He did, however, hope one day to grab a finals MVP trophy to add to his growing collection, for Bryant could never for too long forget individual glory. As he looked toward the start of another season, and possibly a fourth NBA championship, unsettling signs appeared in both Bryant's personal and professional worlds.

Chapter 4

Years of Turmoil

With the Lakers reigning as three-time champions, observers chose them as the team to beat in the 2002–2003 season. A lack of desire shown by some Lakers, however, combined with a flurry of injuries to impede their chances for another title.

No Longer Champions

The Lakers stumbled from the start of the 2002–2003 season. Shaquille O'Neal waited all summer to have toe surgery rather than consulting physicians and having the matter resolved before training camp opened. He was on the bench as the season started. In his absence, the Lakers, plagued with other injuries to key players, won only eleven of their first thirty games. By the end of December, the team faced the possibility that they might not even make it into the playoffs.

Bryant took charge to ensure the Lakers qualified for postseason play. After adding 15 pounds (6.8kg) of muscle in the off-season to increase his durability and to make it easier to pound through the larger forwards and centers who tried to block his path to the basket, Bryant set a new NBA record with twelve 3-pointers in one game, established a new Lakers record by scoring 42 points in a game against Washington, and tallied nine straight games in which he scored 40 or more points. For his feats, Bryant was named the Western Conference Player of the Week five times and Player of the Month in January. By the first part of February, Los Angeles enjoyed a winning record and looked poised to post a winning streak.

With O'Neal returning from his early season surgery and back in top form, and with Bryant orchestrating the offense like a field commander, the Lakers ended with a 50-32 record to advance once again to the playoffs. Bryant was again named to the All-NBA First Team but was more pleased with his selection to the All-NBA Defensive First Team. The nod showed that Bryant concentrated on more than being a scoring machine.

Despite Bryant's accomplishments, the team as a whole was still struggling. Their title hopes ended when the Spurs defeated the Lakers in six games.

Despite Bryant's accomplishments, the team as a whole was still struggling. Accustomed to sweeping aside most first-round playoff opponents, the Lakers needed six games to polish off a scrappy Minnesota Timberwolves squad to advance into a series with the San Antonio Spurs. Their title hopes ended when the Spurs defeated the Lakers in six games, sending Bryant and his teammates off to an early summer.

"We stumbled, we fell, we had inconsistencies, we lacked some discipline as a basketball club—and we paid the price for it,"[56] Phil Jackson said. The Lakers could not overcome the rash of injuries earlier in the season, a drop in focus, and O'Neal's refusal to face surgery during the previous summer.

Nor did some accept the challenges that come with being the NBA champions, as Derek Fisher explained about his Lakers teammates:

It was that kind of year. Nothing really came easy, and I don't know if it should. I don't know if any of our jobs should be easy when you're trying to be the best and be successful over and over again. It shouldn't be easy. It should be that people are willing to step up and take you down and knock you out.

We've done that to everybody else the last three years, and teams got a chance to flip it on us. As much as we taught other teams about getting to this level, we can learn from what happened today as well and come back even better.[57]

Trouble in His Personal Life

Bryant's professional life was not the only area showing strain. His personal life also started to crumble. At the start of 2003, his life off the basketball court seemed to be going well. Bryant and his wife welcomed the birth of their first child, daughter Natalia Diamante Bryant, on January 19, 2003. Teammates noticed a tendency in the new father to bring them into his world, on and off the court, almost as if he felt more comfortable in their presence because he and many of his teammates shared the experience of being fathers.

Taking the Shot

Like every fabled athlete in any sport, Kobe Bryant lives for those times when the game rests in his hands and every eye in the audience is on him. Sometimes he makes the shot or the move and wins the game, while at other times his shot clanks off the rim and the Lakers go home with a defeat. Regardless, he does not shy from seizing the opportunity. He explained his philosophy in a conversation with television interviewer Larry King.

KING: But you like challenge, you like being where the pressure is on you?

BRYANT: Oh, yeah.

KING: You enjoy that?

BRYANT: Absolutely. Absolutely. I mean, you know, life is about challenges. You know, it's about rising. You're not going to succeed every time. Sometimes you fall flat on your face. But it's important to stand up. You might get knocked down, people might trample you, might walk all over you, but you know, stand up, brush it off, keep going.

Quoted in "Transcripts: CNN *Larry King Live.*" CNN.com. January 6, 2005. http://tran scripts.cnn.com/TRANSCRIPTS/0501/06/lkl.01.html.

In an interview with Larry King, Bryant explained his basketball and life philosophies.

The arrival helped restore relations with Bryant's parents as well. In an April 2003 newspaper article, Joe Bryant discussed his feud with his son and his wish that the two would once again be close. Bryant read the story, contacted his father, and invited him to Los Angeles to meet his new granddaughter and attend a Lakers game, which Joe had avoided the past two years.

Other signs indicated that all might not be right in Bryant's family life, however. The Lakers noticed that his wife stopped attending Lakers games, and Bryant's teammates remarked to one another that Bryant had begun flirting with female admirers. Bryant's family, teammates, and fans would soon learn he was doing more than flirting.

Trouble in Colorado

The incident occurred when Bryant arrived at the Lodge and Spa at Cordillera Hotel in Edwards, Colorado, on June 30, 2003, for planned knee surgery. While checking in, he met Katelyn Faber, a nineteen-year-old hotel worker who gave Bryant a tour of the facilities, including the gym and sauna. They flirted a little, and when Bryant later called the front desk to have some food brought up and to have the whirlpool bath checked, Faber offered to go. When Bryant invited the young woman back to his room after she finished her shift, Faber agreed.

Both Bryant and Faber agreed that the two started kissing that night, but disagree about what happened next. Faber claimed Bryant forced her to engage in sexual activities; Bryant claimed she willingly went along. Trina McKay, one of the workers on duty that night, saw Faber after the incident and told police that nothing looked unusual, but a bellman and high school friend of Faber's named Bobby Pietrack claimed his friend appeared to be quite disturbed.

"As we started to walk to the time clock (she) grabbed my arm and started to cry and said that Kobe Bryant choked her," Pietrack informed police. "After we clocked out, I asked her to tell me everything, and that is when she told me that Kobe Bryant had forced sex with her." He added that Faber "was very shaken and she was crying"[58] as the two walked to their cars from the hotel. Faber agreed to go to the police about the matter. She told them that she most likely conveyed to Bryant her wishes to be kissed but that she wanted it to go no further than that.

Unaware of events, the next day Bryant played checkers in the hotel lobby with his bodyguards, then arrived at his physician's medical facility for the surgery. When he returned to the hotel later that afternoon, still groggy from the procedure, he found police waiting to question him. Bryant admitted having sex with Faber but contended that she willingly went along, never objected, and gave him a kiss and asked for his autograph as she left his room. He agreed to provide a DNA sample and to sit for a lie detector test.

On July 4, with Bryant back in Los Angeles, Eagle County sheriff Joseph Hoy issued a warrant for Bryant's arrest. Accompanied by his wife, Bryant returned to Colorado to place himself in police custody and was released on a twenty-five-thousand-dollar bond. That same day, the news media learned of the arrest, causing a torrent of reporters from around the nation to descend on Colorado.

On July 18, the Eagle County district attorney's office filed a formal charge against Bryant for sexual assault. If convicted, the Lakers star faced a prison sentence of four years to life or twenty years on probation, a fine of $750,000, registration as a sex offender, and nullification of his contract with the Lakers.

That same day, Bryant held a press conference. With Vanessa at his side, he admitted to a sexual encounter but denied raping Faber. With tears filling his eyes, Bryant said he loved his wife and that the two of them intended to fight what they saw as a false accusation. Vanessa followed with a statement of support, saying, "I know my husband made a mistake—the mistake of adultery. He and I will have to deal with that."[59]

Lakers teammates could hardly believe the news about a teammate who rarely headed out to nightclubs and who seemed happily married. "I don't know what happened," said teammate Kareem Rush, "but I do know Kobe, and that's not the guy I know."[60] They offered their support to Bryant, but a few mentioned to the press that they wondered if they had ever known the real Kobe Bryant. Athletes throughout the league agreed that

Bryant had compiled a clean-cut image throughout his career, and some added that Bryant's accuser, a college student and former high school cheerleader, was well known among basketball players as a girl who sought the players' attention.

Lakers management fully backed their star. General manager Mitch Kupchak issued a statement saying: "These allegations are completely out of character of the Kobe Bryant we know. For the seven years he's been with us, he has been one of the finest young men we've known and a wonderful asset to both our team and our community. However, since this is a legal matter being handled by the authorities in Colorado, we must refrain from further comment at this time."[61]

Legal Maneuverings

A legal drama ensued, during which prosecuting attorneys gathered and introduced evidence they claimed proved Bryant's guilt, while defense attorneys painted an image of an athlete who mistakenly became involved with a young woman who sought the attention of a famous NBA player. Most legal experts doubted that the district attorney had enough evidence to convict Bryant—the case, after all, boiled down to his word against hers—and wondered if charges would have even been filed had the defendant been anyone but the well-known Lakers guard. Judge Frederick Gannett even warned the district attorney, Mark Hurlbert, that the evidence barely met the legal requirements for filing a charge.

Bryant's attorneys, in an effort to discredit the accuser, asserted that Faber had been taking an antipsychotic drug as treatment for schizophrenia, a psychiatric disorder. One acquaintance claimed that Faber had taken an overdose of pills to commit suicide and that she had been hospitalized four months earlier because of fears that she might do harm to herself. Others admitted that Faber loved being the center of attention and had once unsuccessfully auditioned for *American Idol*, the television show featuring amateur singers. Bryant's legal team tried to plant the notion that she had a pattern of attention-seeking behavior.

In Bryant's trial, prosecuting attorneys gathered and introduced evidence they claimed proved Bryant's guilt, while defense attorneys painted an image of an athlete who mistakenly became involved with a young woman who sought the attention of a famous NBA player.

Most damning, as far as prosecuting attorneys were concerned, was when Fifth Judicial District Court judge Terry Ruckriegle allowed the defense attorneys to bring in evidence of Faber's sexual history during the three days surrounding her encounter with Bryant. The evidence showed that she had engaged in sex with other men in the same time frame as meeting Bryant. If true, Bryant's lawyers intended to argue that Faber willingly entered Bryant's room and agreed to have sex with the star, just as she had done with the other men. Bryant's lawyers were succeeding in gathering evidence that put Faber's believability into question.

A series of errors made by court personnel further complicated the situation. Though guaranteed anonymity, Faber's name was mistakenly posted on the court's website, the transcript of a closed hearing involving Faber mysteriously made its

Willpower

According to television analyst Steve Kerr, one of the top shooters in NBA history and a former teammate of Michael Jordan's, Kobe Bryant exhibited qualities that every great athlete possesses. "It's the will to win, the desire, the absolute undying belief in himself, the arrogance or confidence or whatever you want to call it," he said. "Nobody else playing today has that. Kobe is exactly like Michael [Jordan] when he gets that look in his eye."

Quoted in David DuPree. "Next Up, 100? Strategies, Rule Changes Make It a Possibility." *USA Today*, January 24, 2006. www.usatoday.com/sports/basketball/nba/2006-01-23-100-points_x.htm.

way to news organizations, and a jury questionnaire was leaked to the media. Suddenly, Faber was the center of unwanted attention and now had to deal with the media in addition to the courtroom hearings.

Faber intended to continue with the case despite the notoriety. One of her friends, Sara Dabner, claimed that national attention had nothing to do with Faber's accusations. "Why would a woman put herself through all of this—having people call her names?" Dabner asked. "I think she just wants to see justice done. She's not trying to drag him through the dirt."[62] The media attention, which spiraled into a circus, became overwhelming for Faber. Every news outlet sought information, and tabloid publications plastered the incident across their covers.

Bryant relied on the Lakers organization and a few close friends for support. He said in an interview that he often became scared and distracted during the ordeal, that he was "living in a nightmare and just can't really wake up out of it." He sought the comfort he had always experienced when on the basketball court—the one place where for a few hours he could set aside the turmoil then disrupting his personal life—but even that did not always help focus his mind. "Sometimes it wanders and I have to try to bring myself back to center. It's human nature, I guess,"[63] he said.

Faber's case weakened shortly before the trial was to begin when she admitted lying to police officers about Bryant forcing her to clean herself up before leaving his room. More and more, both sides appeared eager to find a solution to avoid what would most likely be an awkward, embarrassing few months before a jury, one that would magnify the media circus already in fast mode.

An Apology

On September 1, 2004, Bryant's attorneys met with Faber's to conclude an agreement. Although no one knows for certain what unfolded, it appears that in exchange for Faber dropping the charges, Bryant was willing to issue a public apology and to agree to a settlement to avoid a possible civil lawsuit Faber filed. Ruckriegle dismissed the charges that same day, after which Bryant issued an apology to Faber in which he stated his sorrow over the pain both had suffered and that he did not doubt her motives in bringing the charges:

> First, I want to apologize directly to the young woman involved in this incident. I want to apologize to her for my behavior that night and for the consequences she has suffered in the past year. Although this year has been incredibly difficult for me personally, I can only imagine the pain she has had to endure. I also want to apologize to her parents and family members, and to my family and friends and supporters, and to the citizens of Eagle, Colorado.
>
> I also want to make it clear that I do not question the motives of this young woman. No money has been paid to this woman. She has agreed that this statement will not be used against me in the civil case. Although I truly believe this encounter between us was consensual, I recognize now that she did not and does not view this incident the same way I did. After months of reviewing discovery, listening to her attorney, and even her testimony in person, I now

understand how she feels that she did not consent to this encounter.

I issue this statement today fully aware that while one part of this case ends today, another remains. I understand that the civil case against me will go forward. That part of this case will be decided by and between the parties directly involved in the incident and will no longer be a financial or emotional drain on the citizens of the state of Colorado.[64]

District Attorney Hurlbert believed he had enough evidence to convict Bryant and wanted to pursue the case, but with Faber being unwilling to testify, he had no choice but to drop the charges. He explained that the decision occurred after several meetings with Faber's attorney, with Faber's family, and with Faber herself, and that "the victim has informed us, after much of her own labored deliberation, that she does not want to proceed with this trial. For this reason, and this reason only, the case is being dismissed." He added, "This is the victim's personal decision. Candidly, I understand why she had misgivings about her rights being protected."[65]

The rough times, at least on the surface, did not irreparably hamper Bryant's marriage, although most close associates and observers agreed that the union had absorbed some mortifying blows. He knew he had to make amends for dragging his wife through such a public tribulation, and he tried to show his remorse with a purchase of a $4-million diamond ring for his wife. The pair began appearing at public events, such as an outing to Disneyland and to the Teen Choice Awards, and Bryant even joined teammates at a retirement party at Shaquille O'Neal's Beverly Hills mansion for Brian Shaw.

"I've spoken with Kobe several times since this happened," said music executive and Bryant friend Steve Stoute. "He's holding up well. He's a strong guy with confidence in himself and the character not to let this bring him down. He has a focus that's amazing, and he's able to weather anything without it affecting his performance."[66]

Bryant lost some profitable business endorsements in the wake of the accusations, as most companies are deeply conscious

Bryant knew he had to make amends for dragging his wife through such a public tribulation, and he tried to show his remorse by buying a $4-million diamond ring for Vanessa. The pair began appearing at public events, like the 2003 Teen Choice Awards.

of an endorser's public image, but he regained many after the settlement, including deals with Coca-Cola, Nike, and Spalding. Earning $13 million a year from product endorsements, he trails only the Miami Heat's LeBron James.

Women's rights advocates, wanting to ensure that the case ended fairly, closely followed the proceedings. They contended that an injustice would have occurred had the case been dismissed without comment by Bryant, but they took Bryant's apology as a victory for females. He at least admitted that he and Faber held differing views of the evening and was sorry for any pain caused.

As this case unraveled over the course of a year, the Lakers faced an unusual situation on the court. Rather than being the team to beat, they saw their former three-time championship squad crumble. As Bryant's personal world collapsed, the Lakers dynasty neared an end.

Chapter 5

Up and Down Years

The Lakers hoped to reverse the outcome of the past season and once again sweep to another championship trophy in the 2003–2004 season. More injuries and squabbling among team members and with management made that dream more difficult.

2003–2004 Season

The high expectations rested on the arrival in the off-season of All-Stars Karl Malone and Gary Payton. Combined with Bryant and O'Neal, the Lakers featured four All-Stars in their lineup, a potent arsenal that many believed could win most of its games with ease. When the Lakers won twenty-one of their first twenty-six games, that championship seemed a reality.

Injuries to key players halted momentum. Slowed by his knee surgery and worried about his legal troubles, Bryant had trouble finding his rhythm. Karl Malone sat out thirty-nine games with a torn right knee ligament, and Rick Fox, the team's best defensive player, missed forty-four games due to foot problems.

In past years, O'Neal would have picked up the slack, but overweight and still suffering from the lingering effects of his own surgery, he could only help in spurts. Opponents no longer double-teamed O'Neal, giving them a free defender to cover Bryant or one of the other Lakers players.

During the Finals against the Detroit Pistons, the Lakers lost four of the five games. Bryant made only one in three shots during the series.

Turmoil surrounded Bryant when he returned to the court. When teammates and coaches noticed that Bryant returned to his ball-hogging tendencies, Jackson made a point of dropping comments to the press about his selfish style, even once calling Bryant uncoachable. Bryant, already affected by the Colorado case, was offended by the comments and said that while he respected Jackson as a coach, he did not like him as a person.

O'Neal caused more waves by feuding with team owner Jerry Buss about receiving a $100 million extension to his contract, which the owner was reluctant to grant. O'Neal vented his anger at Bryant, saying that the guard sought public adoration and basketball glory, and insulted Lakers general manager Mitch Kupchak by suggesting he was clueless about how to do his job. O'Neal began shouting at crowds during games and told the press that Bryant and his other teammates refused to get the ball to him often enough.

Instead of a unit working together, the Lakers had dissolved into a collection of individuals. Ric Bucher, a writer for *ESPN the Magazine*, examined the team and concluded that "the Lakers never carried themselves like champions the entire season. Too much bickering about their roles. Too much talk by those with an option to leave about being elsewhere. Too many games, particularly in the playoffs, where they were outworked or lost focus. Too much arrogance, even now, about how they're not being beaten but are beating themselves."[67]

Despite the chaos, the Lakers had a 31-19 record by the All-Star break. Bryant was voted as a starter to the team for the sixth consecutive year and scored 20 points to lead all starters. With 24 points and 11 rebounds, however, O'Neal took home the MVP trophy.

With Bryant leading the way, the Lakers won seven of the first eight games after the break, then ended the season by triumphing in fourteen of their final seventeen contests. The team clinched the Pacific Division championship when Bryant drained a 3-point shot at the buzzer to tie Portland, then a second 3-pointer near the end of overtime to win the game.

With a 56-26 record—amazing when one considers the turbulent conditions that swirled about the team—the Lakers were the odds-on favorites to capture the finals. They defeated their first three opponents—the Houston Rockets, San Antonio Spurs, and Minnesota Timberwolves—to earn a spot in the finals against the Detroit Pistons. But the Lakers ran out of steam and lost four of the five games against the Pistons. Bryant made only one in three shots during the series, a subpar performance for the guard.

2004–2005 Season

After the troubled season, Phil Jackson resigned as coach, stating that the feud between his star players was wearing him down. The Lakers signed two-time NBA champion Rudy Tomjanovich to be the new coach.

Lakers management decided to shake things up even more. General manager Mitch Kupchak explained that the Lakers wanted to be younger and quicker in 2004–2005 than they had been and intended to rely on a game that featured fast breaks and quick passes. To that end, the Lakers traded or declined to sign four of their previous starters.

They kicked it off with a giant move. Before the season, Shaquille O'Neal, upset with Jackson's departure and the Lakers' refusal to give him a contract extension and weary of fighting with Bryant, demanded to be traded. Lakers management worried that at age thirty-two, O'Neal had seen his better years, that the center had recently been overweight and out of shape, and that he had struggled with an inability to make free throws, one of the easiest shots in basketball. His ineptness at the free throw line caused other teams to employ the "Hack-a-Shaq" strategy— they simply fouled O'Neal in crucial moments of close games, banking that O'Neal would miss the shots. The Lakers obliged O'Neal's desire to be traded, sending him to the Miami Heat in exchange for Lamar Odom, Caron Butler, Brian Grant, and a first-round draft selection.

The fresh faces made it easier for Bryant to make a decision about whether to stay with the team. The Los Angeles Clippers badly wanted the Lakers star, but with O'Neal gone and new teammates arriving, Bryant re-signed with the Lakers only one day after the team traded O'Neal. "It feels great to be in the city of Los Angeles playing for the Lakers the next seven years,"[68] Bryant said of his $136 million over seven years.

Bryant then had to contend with charges that he orchestrated the entire affair. Critics charged that he nudged out Jackson and O'Neal so he could be the team's unquestioned star. He insisted he had had nothing to do with either man departing. "That upsets me. That angers me. That hurts me," Bryant replied to the

Kobe Battles Kobe

The conflicting themes of individual excellence versus team play have kept reappearing throughout Kobe Bryant's career. He has at times corralled the desire to win every game singlehandedly, while on other occasions his natural inclination to dominate has won out. Allison Samuels, who covered the Lakers for *Newsweek* magazine, wrote about Bryant's inner contradiction early in the 2003–2004 season.

> Selfish is a word lobbed with amazing frequency at the 25-year-old Bryant. Despite being one of basketball's biggest stars, with a boy-next-door demeanor to match, Bryant has suffered from a reputation as an aloof ball hog who doesn't quite know what it means to be a team player. Those close to Bryant—and there are precious few—say what appears to be selfishness is in fact single-mindedness, a laser-like focus on becoming the best basketball player in the world. But the same quality that allowed him to dominate the game at such an astonishingly young age is also his most dangerous weakness. Bryant has been so focused on his career on court, and so sheltered from social development off it, that he may not have picked up some necessary tools in his journey from boy to man, family and friends say.

Allison Samuels. "Kobe Off the Court." *Newsweek*, October 13, 2003. www.newsweek.com/2003/10/12/kobe-off-the-court.html.

charges. "They did what they had to do. That had nothing to do with me. In a perfect world, we would have all come back and won another (championship)." Bryant admitted that relations were strained with both O'Neal and Jackson but said those feelings could easily be set aside. "I even said at the end of the season that I wouldn't mind playing with them for the rest of my career."[69]

A growing number of fans blamed Bryant for breaking up a team that had won three championships, and during the season, sales of Bryant's jersey dropped from its usual spot in the top five. If he were to regain his popular fan base, Bryant would have to help the Lakers back to their winning ways.

More Problems

With Rudy Tomjanovich in charge and the new additions on the floor, the Lakers had compiled a mediocre 15-12 record by the end of December. The only highlight was a Christmas Day match against Shaquille O'Neal and the Miami Heat. Bryant scored a game-high 42 points to best O'Neal's 24, but the Lakers let a fourth quarter lead slip away and lost in overtime.

Bryant suffered another severe ankle sprain in a January contest and missed a month of play. By the All-Star break, the Lakers stood at 22-16, a decent mark but not one that compared with the championship years when Jackson, Bryant, and O'Neal led the team. Conditions had to improve if they were to make the playoffs.

A major distraction occurred when former coach Jackson published a book about the previous season titled *The Last Season: A Team in Search of Its Soul*. He wasted little time making his point that Los Angeles offered one of the most difficult jobs in professional sports by calling the Lakers "the longest-running soap opera in professional sports."[70]

The book included harsh criticism of Bryant. Jackson admitted that the O'Neal-Bryant feud caused him to seek help from a therapist, and he said Bryant's desire to enjoy the spotlight damaged the squad. Jackson claimed he could not trust Bryant and called him an aloof man who declined to become involved with his teammates on and off the court. Whenever he attempted to persuade Bryant to be more of a team player, Bryant sulked. "Kobe can be consumed with surprising anger, which he's displayed toward me and toward his teammates,"[71] wrote Jackson.

The distractions proved too disruptive. The new coach, Tomjanovich, resigned in February, citing poor health as his reason for leaving the team. His 24-19 win-loss record was not bad, but he felt he needed time away from coaching.

Lakers assistant coach Frank Hamblen, who had also worked with Phil Jackson, took over the team for the remainder of the year. A few weeks later, Bryant returned from his injury, but the Lakers never regained the form they had enjoyed during the Bryant-O'Neal years. They fell to a dismal 34-48 record for the year, the worst record since the 1993–1994 season, three years before Bryant joined the team. For the first time in eleven years, the Lakers had been eliminated from postseason play.

Coach Ruby Tomjanovich resigned in February 2005, leaving the Lakers assistant coach Frank Hamblen (right), who had also worked with Phil Jackson, to take over the team for the remainder of the year. For the first time in eleven years, the Lakers had been eliminated from postseason play.

Jackson Returns

The answer to the Lakers' inability to improve lay in the past. After an absence of one year, Phil Jackson agreed to coach the Lakers again. Some doubted that he and Bryant could work together, especially after the publication of Jackson's book, but Bryant immediately dispelled those notions. He said he had already forgotten any negative comments Jackson wrote, and he welcomed the coach back. Assistant coach Brian Shaw, a former Lakers player, claimed that the superstar and coach learned in the year's separation that they actually missed each other and worked together better than they had realized.

The pair was about all that remained from the glory years. In an effort to bring more youth and speed to the lineup, the Lakers, as they had with Bryant, again dipped into the high school market to draft center Andrew Bynum, a highly touted athlete and the youngest selection ever in the NBA draft. They also traded for Kwame Brown from the Washington Wizards and signed free-agent Smush Parker.

Jackson, in a move indicating he believed Bryant had matured from his recent travails, told Bryant that as the team now had so many younger and inexperienced members, he would have to step up and score until the others gained more experience. Bryant never shied from being the focus of a team's offense and readily agreed, but even more to his liking was that his coach, in giving Bryant additional responsibility on the court, had indicated his respect for the player. When the Lakers had Shaquille O'Neal and other veterans, team management had had little inclination to place pressure on a kid right out of high school like Bryant had been. Jackson had turned to O'Neal for leadership, but he now treated Bryant in the same manner.

"I think they both appreciate each other and have a respect for each other that maybe they didn't have before," said Brian Shaw. "Kobe is accepting Phil's coaching and Phil is accepting that Kobe's matured now, so he's giving him more responsibility to do things and say things out there on the floor."[72]

Bryant relished the new approach. In a December game against the Dallas Mavericks, Bryant singlehandedly outscored the opposition through the first three quarters, notching 30

Peace at Last

Hall of Fame Boston Celtic center Bill Russell, who some claim was the greatest defensive player of all time, helped smooth matters between Kobe Bryant and Shaquille O'Neal when he told O'Neal that for the good of the game he should set aside any negative feelings toward Bryant. Before a January 2006 game pitting O'Neal's Miami Heat against Bryant's Lakers, O'Neal approached Bryant and congratulated him on the birth of his daughter. The two shook hands, embraced, and exchanged a few words at center court when the team captains and game officials met before the game, and then hugged again before the opening tip-off.

"It made me feel good," a surprised but pleased Bryant said afterward.

Quoted in "O'Neal Squashes Feud with Bryant." *Washington Post.* January 18, 2006. www.washingtonpost.com/wp-dyn/content/article/2006/01/17/AR2006011701377_pf.html.

Before a game, Shaq approached Bryant and congratulated him on the birth of his daughter. The two former teammates and rivals shook hands, embraced, and exchanged a few words at center court.

points in the third quarter alone. With the game in hand, Jackson sat his veteran guard and allowed the younger players to gain much-needed experience.

In January, he became the first player since Hall of Fame center Wilt Chamberlain in 1964 to record four consecutive games in which he tallied at least 45 points. Adoring Lakers fans cheered Bryant, chanting the nickname he had begun calling himself, Black Mamba, after the legendary snake's ferocious abilities. "The mamba can strike with 99% accuracy at maximum speed, in rapid succession," Bryant told ESPN. "That's the kind of basketball precision I want to have."[73]

Eighty-One Points

Bryant attained that precision on January 22, 2006, against the Toronto Raptors when he scored an incredible 81 points to lead his team to a 122-104 victory. With his team falling behind by 18 points approaching the third quarter, Bryant took over. Teammate Lamar Odom noticed that at halftime the guard was visibly angry with the progress of the game and sat in the locker room without saying a word. Odom guessed by the fierce look in Bryant's eyes that something special was about to unfold.

In one of the most impressive performances in NBA history, Bryant scored 55 points in the second half on his way to a game-high 81, second in NBA history to Wilt Chamberlain's 100-point game in March 1962. After tallying 26 points in the first half, Bryant poured in 27 in the third quarter and 28 in the fourth to outscore the Raptors by 14 points after halftime.

Sportswriter Royce Webb watched the game and labeled it the greatest individual performance in four decades. Webb wrote that as he witnessed Bryant work his magic, the crowd's enthusiasm soared to a height he had never seen. "It was the sound of a crowd at the circus, watching the trapeze artists at work, watching the greatest show on earth."[74]

Absorbed in running his team, Jackson had no idea Bryant approached 80 points until late in the fourth quarter, when assistant Frank Hamblen notified him. Jackson recalled, "I wasn't keeping track on what he had and I turned [to Hamblen] and

Bryant set a personal best on January 22, 2006, against the Toronto Raptors when he scored an incredible 81 points to lead his team to a 122-104 victory. In one of the most impressive performances in NBA history, he scored 55 points in the second half.

said, 'I think I better take him out now.' It was a time I felt the game was sealed, but [Hamblen] said, 'I don't think you can, he has 77 points.' So we stayed with it until he hit 80."[75]

After the game, Jackson, who normally assesses games in an impartial, unemotional manner, left no doubt what he thought of his guard's performance. "I've seen some remarkable games but I've never seen anything like that before," said Jackson, who played against Chamberlain and coached Michael Jordan. "We rode the hot hand."[76]

Observers claimed that Bryant's 81-point game was more impressive than Chamberlain's 100-point game. In 1962 teammates purposely fed the ball to Chamberlain, who shot on every possession. They stepped onto the court determined that their teammate would hit the 100-point mark and did all they could to help him reach the mark. Players declined even to take open shots if they had them in order to get the ball to Chamberlain. Bryant had no such intention. His only purpose was to win the game.

Bryant continued his torrid pace. On March 3, he became the youngest player in NBA history to reach 16,000 points in a career. The next month, he passed former Lakers great Elgin Baylor by notching his twenty-fourth 40-point game of the season. Bryant ended the year with 2,832 points—the seventh-highest total in NBA history. Despite playing with a young supporting cast, Bryant helped the Lakers return to the playoffs.

The young Lakers had a fast exit from the playoffs, where they faced the heavily favored Phoenix Suns in the first round. After splitting the first two games at Phoenix, the Lakers won the next game to go up 2-1 in the best of seven series, then swiped Game 4 when Bryant made a layup with less than one second in regulation time to send the game into overtime. Trailing in overtime by 1 point with only a few seconds remaining, Bryant snared a tipped ball, dribbled down court, and hit a jump shot as time ran out to give the Lakers a 3-1 series lead.

The more experienced Suns, however, forced a Game 7 against the young Lakers by winning the next two contests. Their experience came through during crucial moments, and the Suns handily knocked Bryant and the Lakers out of the playoffs, making the Lakers only the eighth NBA team to lose a series after leading 3-1 in a series.

Though they headed into the summer with a bitter taste in their mouths, the Lakers had much to look forward to. They again had Jackson supervising the team, the young players had gained invaluable experience, and Bryant had proved to be a more mature leader on the court. The next year looked promising.

2006–2007 Season

The return of Phil Jackson had a calming effect on Bryant, who began to understand that championship teams relied on five individuals blending together. Before the next season started, the twenty-eight-year-old Bryant hoped to show that he was not just seeking individual glory. "It's about us getting better, not me being a crutch for us as a team to rely on when we struggle,"[77] he said. He understood that with so many young players on the squad, his work would be difficult, but he was willing to make that transition.

Bryant helped center Bynum improve by offering to watch game films of great NBA centers with him. Together, the pair dissected the moves of men like Bill Russell and Hakeem Olajuwon so that Bynum was better able to block shots. The other team members responded to Bryant's amiability. "Kobe has gone out of his way to help," said Smush Parker. "He's trying. We've noticed."[78]

Bryant had to check the impulse to dominate games when he saw his younger teammates turn the ball over or miss a shot Bryant could have easily made. If they—and along with them, he as well—were to grow as a team, Bryant had to let his teammates make their mistakes and learn from them. "You can see the frustration from time to time," said Gregg Popovich, coach of the San Antonio Spurs. "If they don't complete the play, it's there, on his face. But he's putting his trust in them. He's making more of a concerted effort to touch players, pat them on the back, to engage them. He's been much more outgoing."[79]

To the Playoffs

Bryant served two one-game suspensions for striking opposing players. When he elbowed Spurs guard Manu Ginobili

Individual honors again came Bryant's way as he was named to the All-NBA First Team, the NBA All-Defensive First team, and MVP of the All-Star Game, but more importantly, he had shown in this season that he had grown as a team player.

on January 28, the league handed out the first suspension, claiming his elbow was intentional. Bryant contended the move had been accidental, but he lost an appeal of the decision. Jackson came to his player's defense, but Bryant had to sit out a game. Two months later, a similar occurrence again sent Bryant to the sidelines when he made contact with the face of Minnesota Timberwolves guard Marko Jaric. Despite Jaric's statement that he believed the incident was an accident, the league forced Bryant to miss another contest.

Bryant responded by scoring 65, 50, 60, and 50 points in the next four games, all wins that helped steady a Lakers team that had been in a slump. The young Lakers continued their roller-coaster ride, however, winning a few and losing a few, but finished strong enough to post a 42-40 regular season record, good enough to qualify for the playoffs.

The playoffs lasted a mere five games as the outmanned Lakers lost to the Phoenix Suns and their talented guard, Steve Nash, 4-1. Individual honors again came Bryant's way as he was named to the All-NBA First Team, the NBA All-Defensive First Team, and MVP of the All-Star Game, but more importantly, he had shown in this season that he had grown as a team player.

"He's the most talented player in the league," said Popovich. "He's no longer just an athlete getting points. He's an intelligent player trying to help his team win. He is trying to make that transition to the team player who makes everyone better."[80]

Bryant's fellow players agreed. "I don't know what happened with Kobe in the past," teammate Sasha Vujacic said. "I only know what I see now. I see a leader, a great player who wants to help."[81]

In an indication that he was becoming more aware of what it took to be a great star, Bryant changed his jersey number from the number 8 he had worn to number 24. When asked why, he replied that the number reminded him that to be a complete athlete, one had to focus on it twenty-four hours a day.

In many ways, Bryant was showing that he was becoming a different person on the court. While it made him a better overall player, would that growth in Bryant and that renewed focus result in more championships?

A More Seasoned Bryant

Bryant had made significant advances in becoming a team player since first joining the Lakers.

Some observers wondered, however, if Bryant had not returned to his selfish style of play when, before the 2007–2008 season, he asked the Lakers either to bring in additional talent or trade him. As he would prove throughout the season, though, rather than wanting it for himself, he only sought championships for the Lakers.

Most Valuable Player

Championships motivated Bryant. He was not getting younger, and he saw that if he were to again hold a championship trophy, he would need some assistance. "I want to see us get to a contending level," he said at the time. "I want to see us become a championship contender. It's been a frustrating process for me and I'm sure it's been a frustrating process for all Lakers fans. I'm just hoping we can get to that level. I'm still frustrated. I'm waiting for them to make some changes."[82] When the team brought back Derek Fisher, who had played for the Golden State Warriors the previous two years, they fielded a solid nucleus with Bryant, Fisher, Lamar Odom, and Andrew Bynum.

Unlike many players who are content having a solid NBA career, Bryant still wanted to win championships. Some athletes carry a reputation for turning on the effort only when the spotlight shines on them, such as in big games or at the All-Star Game, but Bryant never loses the intensity, the love for competing. "Kobe wants it so badly that he rubs an awful lot of people the wrong way," explained Tex Winter, a Lakers consultant. "But they're not willing to understand what's inside the guy."[83] A *Sports Illustrated* poll of NBA players taken early in the season named Bryant as the runaway winner of the poll of whom the opponent players feared the most.

That competitive edge led Bryant to ask Nike, the maker of his shoes, to shave a few millimeters from the bottom of both

Bryant picked up one honor he had long wanted when in May 2008 he was named the NBA's Most Valuable Player.

shoes because he believed it handed him a hundredth of a second faster reaction time on the court, which in turn could lead to improved play. He often grabbed teammates after practice and studied film with them, illustrating different moves they might attempt that would result in easier shots. Odom and Bynum began studying film more frequently because they saw how well-prepared Bryant was for each contest.

With Bryant's leadership and his young teammates' contributions, the Lakers spurted to a 25-11 record before injuries, including a season-ending knee injury to Bynum, slowed the pace. To offset the injuries, the team acquired center Pau Gasol from the Memphis Grizzlies. Gasol, who instantly took charge under the basket and fed passes to open teammates, loved Jackson's triangle offense. Fueled by Gasol's talents and Bryant's scoring touch, the Lakers snared the Western Conference title.

Bryant picked up one honor he had long wanted when in May 2008 he was named as the NBA's Most Valuable Player. In easily outdistancing the second-place finisher, New Orleans guard Chris Paul, Bryant became the fourth Laker to earn the award, joining Kareem Abdul-Jabbar, Magic Johnson, and Shaquille O'Neal. Reflective of the nature of the trophy, which recognizes a player's total contributions to his team, Bryant's overall scoring average dipped, but his defense, rebounding, and assists improved.

Jackson, the coach who witnessed Bryant's basketball maturation in his years with the Lakers, praised the selection. "I don't know anybody who's ever deserved this trophy more. I've never known anybody that's worked as hard to accomplish what he's accomplished in this game."[84]

It was a dream come true for Bryant, who on the courts in Italy as a youth imagined winning the NBA Finals and a Most Valuable Player Award. "I get goose bumps thinking about it," he said. "It's been a long ride, coming in here at 17 years old and standing here almost 30. I'm an old man. I have tendinitis. I've been through all the wars. I'm very proud to represent this organization, to represent this city."[85] He added that only one thing would make the year perfect—another championship for the Lakers.

Clutch Kobe

Another honor came Kobe Bryant's way when the *Sporting News* named the Lakers guard the NBA player of the decade, a span that offered some of the game's most talented athletes. Shaquille O'Neal, who had battled with Bryant during their hectic days together as Lakers teammates, could not deny the impact of a player like Bryant. He said after learning of Bryant's award:

> The thing about Kobe is that, over the course of my career, I have never played with anyone who was as fierce as he is. If we would go into the fourth quarter, playoffs or just some game in the season and we were within a little bit of the other team, Kobe was not going to shy away from the challenge of getting the win.

Quoted in Houston Mitchell. "Kobe Bryant Is Named NBA Player of the Decade." *Los Angeles Times,* September 24, 2009. http://latimesblogs.latimes.com/sports_blog/2009/09/kobe-bryant-is-named-nba-player-of-the-decade.html.

*The **Sporting News** named the Lakers guard the NBA player of the decade, a span that offered some of the game's most talented athletes.*

The Lakers looked as if they might march to the finals with easy series wins over Denver, Utah, and San Antonio, but the potent Boston Celtics halted their run, taking the trophy in Game 6 with a 131-92 massacre, the largest margin of victory in a championship clincher in NBA history. Bryant made only seven of twenty-two shots in the game, but he was far from the only ineffective player. Bryant later contended that the Boston defense was the best he had seen in the playoffs.

He believed the Lakers would be back for another run the next season. His younger teammates had gained valuable experience during the year, and in Bryant, Gasol, Fisher, Bynum, and Odom, the Lakers fielded a unit as gifted as any in the league.

Olympic Gold

Another highlight of 2008 for Bryant was being selected as a member of the U.S. Olympic basketball team. He joined LeBron James, Dwayne Wade, Chris Bosh, and Jason Kidd on a squad coached by college basketball's most acclaimed coach, Duke University's Mike Krzyzewski.

In August 2008, the United States opened play with a game against China. The NBA athletes had little trouble for most of the Olympics, winning their first seven games by an average margin of 30 points.

The championship game against Spain proved to be different. A tough Spanish squad kept the game close and trailed the United States by only 4 points with less than three minutes remaining. Bryant stepped up his game in the last minutes, however, by draining a 3-point basket and making a subsequent foul shot to increase their lead. The U.S. team held on for a 118-107 victory, the first gold medal in basketball for the United States since the 2000 Olympic Games. Bryant joined James and the others for a wild celebration at midcourt, dancing to Bruce Springsteen's "Born in the U.S.A." and high-fiving everyone. Bryant now had an MVP and a gold medal to add to his growing collection.

2008–2009 Season

Spurred by memories of the blowout loss to the Celtics in Game 6 of the finals the previous season, the Lakers played as if possessed by demons. They won the season's first seven games, won fourteen of the first fifteen, and entered the midseason All-Star break with a 42-10 record, good for the Western Conference lead.

When Bynum went down with a knee injury, Bryant picked up the slack, helping them to crucial wins over Boston and Cleveland along the way to entering the playoffs once again. Bryant approached the postseason with renewed focus on capturing another championship, something that fans and critics had claimed he would never attain without Shaquille O'Neal. Bryant rarely joked or smiled, with the press or his teammates. "I was just locked in, completely locked in," Bryant said. "It's a matter of understanding the moment. It's also understanding your team and the lead that they have to follow. That's what I tried to do. I was grumpy for a while."[86]

A speedy 4-1 series win over the Utah Jazz led to a hard-fought 4-3 series victory against the Houston Rockets and Rockets player Ron Artest for the Western Conference title. The next opponent, the Denver Nuggets, rallied to take Game 2 at Los Angeles, but in Denver Bryant scored 41 points to help the team regain the series lead. They closed out the series in Game 6, 119-92, with Bryant dishing out 10 assists.

The Lakers faced the Orlando Magic for the NBA championship. The Lakers swept the first two games before losing to the Magic in Game 3. The Lakers then raced to a 3-1 series lead by taking Game 4 in Orlando in overtime. Bolstered by the dramatic win, the Lakers took Game 5, 99-86, riding on Bryant's astounding 30 points, 6 rebounds, 5 assists, and 4 blocked shots to snag the trophy. The triumph was the fifteenth such championship in Lakers history and the tenth ring for Jackson, moving him beyond the legendary Boston Celtics coach Red Auerbach into first place.

For his finals play, in which Bryant averaged 32 points, 7 assists, and 6 rebounds per game, Bryant was named the NBA Fi-

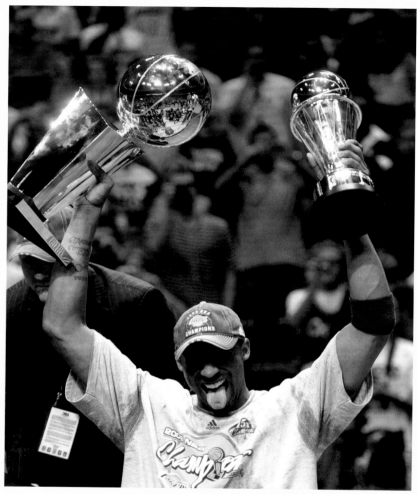

During the Finals, Bryant averaged 32 points, 7 assists, and 6 rebounds per game. He was named the Finals Most Valuable Player for the first time in his career.

nals Most Valuable Player for the first time in his career. The honor, which recognizes the top player in the finals as opposed to the NBA's regular season MVP award, which Bryant had won the year before, not only illustrated Bryant's concentration on team play, but quieted any chatter that he could never win without Shaquille O'Neal. It also helped restore some balance to a life that had been rocked by the Colorado incident and subsequent legal maneuverings, the dismantling of the Jackson-O'Neal-Bryant title team, failure to make the playoffs in 2005, embarrassing first-round playoff exits at the hands of the Phoenix Suns, and a humiliating loss to the Boston Celtics. "It felt like a big old monkey was off my back," Bryant said of the championship. "It felt so good to be able to have this moment."[87]

Jackson aptly summed up what the moment meant for his star guard, a player he believed would never reach his full potential until he learned to put the team above individual honors. He said that, throughout the playoffs, Bryant was the engine that created shots for teammates with accurate passes and scrambling for rebounds and loose balls. He added that Bryant finally learned after all those frustrating seasons "that he had to give to get back in return. He's become a giver rather than just a guy that's a demanding leader, and that's been great for him and great to watch."[88]

2009–2010 Season

Bryant continued his outstanding play the following season. The Lakers entered the All-Star break with a 41-13 record, good enough for the lead in the Western Conference. The personal highlight for Bryant occurred January 21, 2010, when he became only the fifteenth player—and the youngest—in NBA history to reach 25,000 career points. Former Lakers center Kareem Abdul-Jabbar tops the most-career-points list with 38,387.

A December injury, when a ball smashed into his right index finger and fractured it, caused considerable pain, but Bryant declined to be taken out of games. He played for the rest of the season despite considerable discomfort to a crucial part of his shooting hand.

"The first places players can show leadership is where they make the sacrifices, show the sacrifices," Jackson said. "In our situation, Kobe has been playing through injuries that on other teams in other situations players might take two to three weeks off. That tells people this is a team on a mission, that it's not just a job, it's a job that requires sacrifice."[89]

Bryant's ability to focus at crucial moments, even though he battled the damaged finger, shone as the season unfolded. He notched six last-second game-winning shots in the march to the playoffs. Twice in December—against the Miami Heat and the Milwaukee Bucks—he lifted his team to victory in the final seconds. He repeated that with two more in January, sending both the Sacramento Kings and the Boston Celtics home with painful last-second losses, added a fifth in February against the Memphis Grizzlies, and another in March to snatch a 109-107 win over the Toronto Raptors, who put two defenders on Bryant in a vain effort to stop what they knew would be the game-winning attempt. "That's my responsibility here, to close things out,"[90] said Bryant.

Bryant's heroics helped the Lakers to a regular season record of 57-25, enough to again earn the Western Conference title. They also convinced the Lakers to offer a three-year contract extension for $90 million to keep Bryant in Los Angeles through the 2013–2014 season.

With the contract, Bryant became an oddity in the league—unlike other players, who move from team to team, he has played every game in his career with one team. Said general manager Mitch Kupchak:

> My position all along is Kobe started as a Laker and should end his career as a Laker so in my mind I always thought he'd end up as a Laker and we're fairly assured he will end his career as a Laker. Of course, in four years he'll be 35 years old and maybe we'll go through this again but I think at that point after all the years if he did choose to play some more he would choose to play in Los Angeles.[91]

The Lakers also had other key members signed through 2013, including Pau Gasol, Ron Artest, Lamar Odom, and Andrew Bynum—mostly the same team that grabbed the championship the year before. The future for Lakers fans looked rosy indeed.

Before looking ahead to the future, though, the Lakers had to take care of business in the playoffs. They handled their first three rivals—the Oklahoma City Thunder, the Utah Jazz, and the Phoenix Suns—winning twelve of sixteen contests to ad-

A personal highlight for Bryant occurred January 21, 2010, when he became only the fifteenth player—and the youngest—in NBA history to reach 25,000 career points.

He Learns from the Best

To step up to the next level, one that few athletes attain, Bryant turned to the man most people compared him with—Michael Jordan. Bryant said:

> Michael has told me before, "You have all the tools. The mental part of how to elevate your teammates is the last piece you have to master." I find [getting players involved] requires me to be more focused than usual. When I'm scoring, I have a narrow, laser focus. I get totally lost in the rhythm of shooting. But when I'm facilitating, I have to take a step back and look at a much broader picture. I have to wait for things to develop, or make them develop. It takes patience.

Quoted in Jackie MacMullan. "The Transformation of Kobe Bryant." ESPN.com, February 5, 2007. http://sports.espn.go.com/nba/columns/story?columnist=macmullan_jackie&id=2755078.

vance to the finals. "Kobe's so good," said Odom, "he makes incredible normal for us."[92]

Repeating as champions would not be as easy. Their opponent, the venerable Boston Celtics, featured a bruising defense and physical game. Everyone expected a battle to unfold, as the NBA Finals pitted two of the league's most revered organizations in NBA history, and the Lakers still smarted from the embarrassing loss the Celtics had inflicted on them in the 2008 finals.

The opponents lived up to the billing. After splitting the first two games, played in Los Angeles, the teams headed to Boston for three crucial games in Massachusetts. The Lakers took a one-game advantage by swiping Game 3, but then dropped the next two contests to a determined Celtics squad. Bryant and the Lakers returned to Los Angeles, needing victories in the last two games to gain the trophy.

A sterling defensive effort by the Lakers gained a decisive 89-67 win in Game 6, setting up Game 7 for the title. After falling behind by 13 points in the third quarter, mainly due to miserable shooting from Bryant and the rest of the team, the Lakers stormed ahead on the strength of 3-point baskets from Derek Fisher and Ron Artest and the all-around play of Bryant and Gasol. Bryant shook off his cold shooting hand by pouring in 10 points in the final quarter, and the Lakers captured another defensive duel, 83-79 to earn their second consecutive NBA crown.

Bryant later admitted that for the game's first three quarters, he had been trying too hard to make things happen. Errant shots and inaccurate passes frustrated him, but unlike earlier in his career, when he made matters worse by continuing to press, he now stepped back and turned to his passing and defense to help the team. Then, in the final quarter, he regained that magical shooting touch that led to the six game-winning baskets in the regular season. Jackson later praised Bryant for recognizing that during a game in which the shots were not falling for him, he could still help the team in other ways.

Bryant's playoff averages of 29 points, 6 rebounds, and almost 6 assists per game gained him another NBA Finals Most Valuable Player Award. With his fifth ring, Bryant tied with Magic Johnson and moved to within one of Michael Jordan's six championships. More importantly, at least to Bryant, it moved him one ahead of his former teammate. "I got one more than Shaq," a delighted Bryant said to reporters after the game. "And you can take that to the bank."[93]

2010–2011 Season

As the 2010–2011 season approached, Bryant appeared to have gained a balance in his life that he once lacked. He has reopened ties with his parents and sisters, repaired the damage to his marriage caused by the events in Colorado in 2003–2004, and tailored his game to fit better with his teammates.

Bryant has increased his charitable activities off the court as well. He is closely associated with the After-School All-Stars (ASAS), an American nonprofit organization that provides after-school programs to disadvantaged children in different U.S.

cities. Recognizing his immense popularity in China, where basketball enjoys a passionate following and where Bryant is featured in a Chinese reality television program during which he observes and advises Chinese basketball athletes, Bryant has also organized the Kobe Bryant China Fund, a charity to raise money within China earmarked for education and health programs.

The popularity on the court that faded in 2003 has been restored. Bryant's jersey continues to rank among the most popular with fans, rivaling those of LeBron James and Steve Nash. In early November 2010, Bryant became the youngest player in NBA history to record 26,000 career points. At a November 17, 2010, game in Detroit against the Pistons, hometown fans began chanting "MVP" when Bryant had the ball, indicating their assessment that they were watching the game's best player. He gave them their money's worth that night, as he has so often

Recognizing his immense popularity in China, Bryant organized the Kobe Bryant China Fund, a charity to raise money within China earmarked for education and health programs.

before, by scoring 33 points in only thirty-two minutes of play. The Lakers headed into 2011 with a 20-7 record and a solid lead over the second-place Phoenix Suns.

The young boy who spent hours alone on Italian basketball courts, practicing game-winning shots and moves to confound opposing defenders, had learned that a team is much more than its top star. Gradually, the message high school coach Gregg Downer and Phil Jackson had tried to instill became clear. Bryant admitted as much in late 2010. As he stood at the scorer's table to be re-inserted into a game to replace Shannon Brown, Bryant had second thoughts. Brown was on a hot streak, draining baskets with ease. Whereas in the past Bryant may have wanted to return, this time he willingly occupied a backseat to the younger player and told Jackson to leave Brown in the game.

"Now I understand," said Bryant of allowing a teammate to stay on the court while he sat out. "Let him go. Let him ride that. Back in my younger days, I never would've thought about that."[94] This, however, was not the same Kobe Bryant who first entered the NBA. He was a more mature player, willing to share the spotlight with teammates.

Introduction: A Boy's Dream

1. Quoted in Joe Layden. *Kobe: The Story of the NBA's Rising Young Star*. New York: HarperPaperbacks, 1998, p. 12.

Chapter 1: Origins of a Champion

2. Quoted in Layden. *Kobe*, p. 13.
3. Quoted in Jason Levin. "I Wish People Would Let Me Just Be Kobe." *Basketball Digest*, March 2001. http://findarticles .com/p/articles/mi_m0FCJ/is_5_28/ai_71187958.
4. Quoted in Allison Samuels. "Kobe Goes It Alone." *Newsweek*, May 31, 1999. www.newsweek.com/1999/05/30/kobe-goes-it-alone.html.
5. Quoted in Layden. *Kobe*, p. 14.
6. Quoted in Ian Thomsen. "Showtime!" *Sports Illustrated*, April 27, 1998. http://sportsillustrated.cnn.com/vault/ article/magazine/MAG1012689/index.htm.
7. Quoted in Levin. "I Wish People Would Let Me Just Be Kobe."
8. Quoted in Layden. *Kobe*, p. 16.
9. Quoted in Jackie MacMullan. "Kobe Bryant: Imitating Great-ness." ESPN.com, June 4, 2010. http://sports.espn.go.com/ nba/playoffs/2010/columns/story?columnist=macmullan_ jackie&page=kobefilmstudy-100604.
10. Quoted in Thomsen. "Showtime!"
11. Quoted in Chris Ballard. "Kobe's Well-Honed Killer In-stinct." *Sports Illustrated*, May 28, 2008. http://sportsillus trated.cnn.com/vault/article/web/COM1138889/index.htm.
12. Quoted in Layden. *Kobe*, p. 12.
13. Quoted in Allison Samuels. "Kobe Off the Court." *News-week*, October 13, 2003. www.newsweek.com/2003/10/12/ kobe-off-the-court.html.
14. Quoted in Justin Verrier. "Before They Were Stars: Kobe Bryant." ESPN.com, June 1, 2010. http://sports.espn.go.

com/nba/playoffs/2010/columns/story?page=beforethey
werestars-kobe-100601.

15. Quoted in Thomsen. "Showtime!"
16. Quoted in Ballard. "Kobe's Well-Honed Killer Instinct."
17. Quoted in Verrier. "Before They Were Stars."
18. Quoted in Layden. *Kobe*, p. 22.
19. Quoted in Layden. *Kobe*, p. 25.
20. Quoted in Samuels. "Kobe Off the Court."
21. Quoted in Samuels. "Kobe Off the Court."
22. Quoted in Ballard. "Kobe's Well-Honed Killer Instinct."
23. Quoted in Layden. *Kobe*, p. 35.
24. Quoted in Dave McMenamin. "Kobe's Shooting Through
    the Pain." ESPN.com, April 17, 2010. http://sports.espn
    .go.com/los-angeles/nba/columns/story?id=5104918.

Chapter 2: Kobe the Professional

25. Quoted in Layden. *Kobe*, p. 50.
26. Quoted in Michael Bamberger. "School's Out." *Sports Illus-
    trated*, May 6, 1996. http://sportsillustrated.cnn.com/vault/
    article/magazine/MAG1008078/index.htm#ixzz15cxpJhQj.
27. Quoted in Bamberger. "School's Out."
28. Quoted in Layden. *Kobe*, p. 55.
29. Quoted in Verrier. "Before They Were Stars."
30. Quoted in Layden. *Kobe*, p. 66.
31. Quoted in Layden. *Kobe*, p. 81.
32. Quoted in Layden. *Kobe*, p. 83.
33. Quoted in MacMullan. "Kobe Bryant."
34. Quoted in Samuels. "Kobe Goes It Alone."
35. Quoted in Samuels. "Kobe Off the Court."
36. Quoted in Samuels. "Kobe Off the Court."
37. Quoted in Allison Samuels. "Shaq's Side of the Story." *News-
    week*, July 26, 2004. www.newsweek.com/2004/07/25/
    basketball-shaq-s-side-of-the-story.html.
38. Quoted in Samuels. "Kobe Off the Court."
39. Quoted in Samuels. "Kobe Off the Court."
40. Quoted in Thomsen. "Showtime!"
41. Quoted in Layden. *Kobe*, p. 146.
42. Quoted in Samuels. "Kobe Goes It Alone."
43. Quoted in Samuels. "Kobe Goes It Alone."

Chapter 3: A Championship Team

44. Quoted in John Leland. "My White Father." *Newsweek*, June 19, 2000. www.newsweek.com/2000/06/18/my-white-father.html.
45. Quoted in Allison Samuels. "Shaq in the Battle Again." *Newsweek*, April 24, 2000. www.newsweek.com/2000/04/23/shaq-in-the-battle-again.html.
46. Quoted in Scoop Jackson. "Kobe Bryant's Top Ten Moments." ESPN.com, May 8, 2009. http://sports.espn.go.com/espn/page2/story?id=4152884.
47. Quoted in Bill Plaschke. "That Was No Dream, That Was Kobe." *Los Angeles Times*, June 15, 2000. http://articles.la times.com/2000/jun/15/sports/sp-41173.
48. Quoted in Plaschke. "That Was No Dream, That Was Kobe."
49. Quoted in Plaschke. "That Was No Dream, That Was Kobe."
50. Quoted in Ballard. "Kobe's Well-Honed Killer Instinct."
51. Quoted in Allison Samuels. "Kobe: Thanks for Sharing." *Newsweek*. June 4, 2001. www.newsweek.com/2001/06/03/kobe-thanks-for-sharing.html.
52. Quoted in Samuels. "Kobe: Thanks for Sharing."
53. Quoted in Samuels. "Kobe Off the Court."
54. Quoted in NBA.com. "Kobe Continues to Be Thorn in Spurs' Side." May 12, 2002. www.nba.com/games/20020512/LALSAS/recap.html.
55. Quoted in David DuPree. "Bryant's Heroics, Deference Pay Off for Lakers." *USA Today*, June 14, 2002. www.usatoday.com/sports/nba/02playoffs/2002-06-14-kobe.htm.

Chapter 4: Years of Turmoil

56. Quoted in Marc Stein. "Lakers, Spurs Deserved What They Got in Game 6." ESPN.com, May 16, 2003. http://sports.espn.go.com/nba/playoffs2003/story?id=1554599.
57. Quoted in Stein. "Lakers, Spurs Deserved What They Got in Game 6."
58. Quoted in Lauren Johnston. "Kobe Records Released." CBS News, October 1, 2004. www.cbsnews.com/stories/2004/08/16/national/main636205.shtml.

59. Quoted in Allison Samuels. "Who Is the Real Kobe?" *Newsweek*, July 28, 2003. www.newsweek.com/2003/07/27/who-is-the-real-kobe.print.html.

60. Quoted in Allison Samuels. "A Tough Summer—and Maybe a Hard Fall—for Kobe." *Newsweek*, July 21, 2003. www.newsweek.com/2003/07/20/a-tough-summer-and-maybe-a-hard-fall-for-kobe.html.

61. Quoted in "Woman Accuses Lakers Star of Sexual Misconduct." Denver Channel.com. July 6, 2003. www.thedenverchannel.com/sports/2314127/detail.html.

62. Quoted in "Friend Says Kobe's Accuser 'Felt Chemistry' with NBA Star." Denver Channel.com. July 23, 2003. www.thedenverchannel.com/sports/2351952/detail.html.

63. Quoted in "Bryant Distracted, Scared Amid Sex Assault Case." *Sports Illustrated*. December 26, 2003. http://sportsillustrated.cnn.com/2003/basketball/nba/12/26/kobe.interview.ap/index.html?cnn-yes.

64. Quoted in "Kobe Bryant's Apology." ESPN.com. September 1, 2004. http://sports.espn.go.com/nba/news/story?id=1872928.

65. Quoted in T. R. Reid. "Bryant Rape Case Ends in Dismissal." *Washington Post*, September 2, 2004. www.sfgate.com/cgibin/article.cgi?file=/c/a/2004/09/02/MNG6E8IB861.DTL.

66. Quoted in Samuels. "Kobe Off the Court."

Chapter 5: Up and Down Years

67. Ric Bucher. "Lakers' Wrongs Making Things Right." ESPN.com, June 15, 2004. http://sports.espn.go.com/nba/playoffs2004/columns/story?columnist=bucher_ric&id=1822275.

68. Quoted in "Kobe Remains with Lakers." ESPN.com. July 15, 2004. http://sports.espn.go.com/nba/news/story?id=1840336.

69. Quoted in "Kobe Remains with Lakers."

70. Phil Jackson with Michael Arkush. *The Last Season: A Team in Search of Its Soul*. New York: Penguin, 2004, p. 35.

71. Jackson. *The Last Season*, p. 10.

72. Quoted in Howard Beck. "Coach and Star Savor Success in Collaboration." *New York Times*, May 6, 2006. www.nytimes.com/2006/05/06/sports/basketball/06lakers.html?_r=1.

73. Quoted in Jerry Crowe. "Text Messages from Press Row...." *Los Angeles Times*, May 23, 2008. http://articles.latimes.com/2008/may/23/sports/sp-crowe23.

74. Royce Webb. "Kobe Makes Records Wilt." ESPN.com, January 23, 2006. http://sports.espn.go.com/nba/dailydime?page=dailydime-060123.

75. Quoted in "Eighty-One! Bryant Erupts as Lakers Roll." NBA.com. January 22, 2006. www.nba.com/games/20060122/TORLAL/recap.html.

76. Quoted in "Eighty-One! Bryant Erupts as Lakers Roll."

77. Quoted in Jackie MacMullan. "The Transformation of Kobe Bryant." ESPN.com, February 5, 2007. http://sports.espn.go.com/nba/columns/story?columnist=macmullan_jackie&id=2755078.

78. Quoted in MacMullan. "The Transformation of Kobe Bryant."

79. Quoted in MacMullan. "The Transformation of Kobe Bryant."

80. Quoted in MacMullan. "The Transformation of Kobe Bryant."

81. Quoted in MacMullan. "The Transformation of Kobe Bryant."

Chapter 6: A More Seasoned Bryant

82. Quoted in "Kobe Wants West to Return to Lakers with Full Authority." ESPN.com. May 27, 2007. http://sports.espn.go.com/nba/news/story?id=2884339.

83. Quoted in Ballard. "Kobe's Well-Honed Killer Instinct."

84. Quoted in Mike Bresnahan. "His Day Is Letter-Perfect." *Los Angeles Times*, May 7, 2008. http://articles.latimes.com/2008/may/07/sports/sp-lakers7.

85. Quoted in Bresnahan. "His Day Is Letter-Perfect."

86. Quoted in Jeff Zillgitt. "Man on a Mission: Bryant Revels in Victory, Finals MVP." *USA Today*, June 16, 2009. www.usatoday.com/sports/basketball/nba/2009-06-15-bryant-finals-mvp_N.htm.

87. Quoted in J. A. Adande. "Journey Complete: Kobe Leads Lakers to NBA Championship." June 15, 2009. http://sports.espn.go.com/nba/dailydime?page=dime-090615.

88. Quoted in Zillgitt. "Man on a Mission."

89. Quoted in Frank Fitzpatrick. "Bryant No Hero in His Hometown of Philly." *Philadelphia Inquirer*, January 29, 2010. www.philly.com/philly/sports/sixers/83010232.html.

90. Quoted in Greg Beacham. "Lakers Snap 3-Game Skid on Bryant's Late Jumper." March 10, 2010. http://sports .yahoo.com/nba/recap;_ylt=AlE2BVZ0w4mrHxy_lzrfziy 8vLYF?gid=2010030913.

91. Quoted in "Bryant Signs for 3 Years, Nearly $90M." ESPN .com. April 2, 2010. http://sports.espn.go.com/los-angeles/ nba/news/story?id=5050933.

92. Quoted in "Lakers Beat Suns to Set Up Rematch with Boston." *Sporting News*. May 30, 2010. www.sportingnews .com/nba/story/2010-05-29/lakers-beat-suns-set-rematch-boston.

93. Quoted in Sekou Smith. "No Doubt About the MVP." *Hang Time Blog*, June 18, 2010. http://hangtime.blogs.nba .com/2010/06/18/no-doubt-about-the-mvp/?ls=iref:nbahpt1.

94. Quoted in Terry Foster. "King of Pop Proved a Mentor to Kobe Bryant." *Detroit News*, November 25, 2010. http://det news.com/article/20101125/OPINION03/11250320/1127/ sports/King-of-Pop-proved-a-mentor-to-Kobe-Bryant.

Important Dates

1978

On August 23, Kobe Bryant is born in Philadelphia, Pennsylvania.

1984

The Bryants move to Italy.

1991

The Bryants return to the Philadelphia area.

1996

Kobe Bryant leads his high school team to a state championship; he is named the Naismith and the Gatorade High School Player of the Year; on April 29 he announces his decision to skip college and enter the professional draft; on June 16 he is drafted by the Charlotte Hornets and later obtained by the Los Angeles Lakers.

2000

Wins his first NBA championship.

2001

Marries Vanessa Laine on April 18; wins his second NBA championship.

2002

Wins his third NBA championship.

2003

On January 19 daughter Natalia Diamante is born; on July 4 a warrant is issued for Kobe Bryant's arrest on sexual assault charges; on July 18 formal charges are filed.

2004

The case against Bryant is dismissed on September 1; he signs an agreement with the other involved party and issues an apology.

2006

Scores 81 points on January 22 against the Toronto Raptors to post the second-highest total in one game in NBA history; on May 1 daughter Gianna Maria-Onore is born.

2008

Receives the NBA's Most Valuable Player Award; wins an Olympic gold medal as part of the U.S. team.

2009

Wins his fourth NBA championship; is named the NBA Finals Most Valuable Player.

2010

Becomes the youngest player in NBA history to reach 25,000 career points; wins his fifth NBA championship; is again named the NBA Finals Most Valuable Player; signs an extension to his contract guaranteeing his play for the Lakers through the 2013–2014 season.

Books

Matt Christopher. *On the Court with Kobe Bryant*. Boston: Little, Brown, 2001. The popular writer of books for students delivers a solid biography of the Lakers star.

Phil Jackson with Michael Arkush. *The Last Season: A Team in Search of Its Soul*. New York: Penguin, 2004. Jackson gives one of the most interesting glimpses of a professional basketball season in this memoir. He also explains the methods he uses to be a successful coach.

Mike Krzyzewski with Jamie K. Spatola. *The Gold Standard: Building a World-Class Team*. New York: Business Plus, 2009. The coach of the gold medal–winning 2008 U.S. Olympic Team, of which Bryant was a part, shows how he assembled the team and succeeded in molding personalities like Bryant into a unified squad.

Joe Layden. *Kobe: The Story of the NBA's Rising Young Star*. New York: HarperPaperbacks, 1998. Layden's book provides an in-depth examination of Bryant's high school and early professional career and features player and coach interviews.

Roland Lazenby. *Mad Game: The NBA Education of Kobe Bryant*. Chicago: Masters, 2000. This is a fine source of information about the early portion of Bryant's life.

Pat Mixon. *The Kobe Code: Eight Principles for Success*. North Charleston, SC: CreateSpace, 2010. The author uses Bryant's life to illustrate how people can succeed, mainly by applying eight guiding concepts Bryant follows. Among the principles are to master your craft and have a passion for what you do.

Jeff Savage. *Kobe Bryant*. Minneapolis: Lerner, 2003. Part of the publisher's series of biographies for young readers, Savage's book shows how Bryant used his early experiences to take him to the NBA.

Jeffrey Scott Shapiro and Jennifer Stevens. *Kobe Bryant: The Game of His Life*. New York: Revolution, 2004. The authors examine Bryant's 2003 Colorado incident and the legal steps that followed the accusations against Bryant.

Internet Sources

J. A. Adande. "Journey Complete: Kobe Leads Lakers to NBA Championship." ESPN.com, June 15, 2009. http://sports.espn .go.com/nba/dailydime?page=dime-090615.

Chris Ballard. "Kobe's Well-Honed Killer Instinct." *Sports Illustrated*, May 28, 2008. http://sportsillustrated.cnn.com/vault/ article/web/COM1138889/index.htm.

Michael Bamberger. "School's Out." *Sports Illustrated*, May 6, 1996. http://sportsillustrated.cnn.com/vault/article/maga zine/MAG1008078/index.htm#ixzz15cxpJhQj.

Howard Beck. "Coach and Star Savor Success in Collaboration." *New York Times*, May 6, 2006. www.nytimes.com/2006/05/06/ sports/basketball/06lakers.html?_r=1.

Jerry Crowe. "Text Messages from Press Row...." *Los Angeles Times*, May 23, 2008. http://articles.latimes.com/2008/ may/23/sports/sp-crowe23.

John Delong. "Lakers' Trade for Bryant Has Been Misconstrued." *Winston-Salem (NC) Journal*, June 18, 2008. www2.journal now.com/sports/2008/jun/18/lakers-trade-for-bryant-has- been-misconstrued-ar-113126.

Frank Fitzpatrick. "Bryant No Hero in His Hometown of Philly." *Philadelphia Inquirer*, January 29, 2010. www.philly.com/ philly/sports/sixers/83010232.html.

Scoop Jackson. "Kobe Bryant's Top Ten Moments." ESPN. com, May 8, 2009. http://sports.espn.go.com/espn/page2/ story?id=4152884.

Jackie MacMullan. "The Transformation of Kobe Bryant." February 5, 2007. http://sports.espn.go.com/nba/columns/ story?columnist=macmullan_jackie&id=2755078.

Arash Markazi. "Youngest to 26K." November 12, 2010. http:// espn.go.com/los-angeles/kobe/index?postId=5794855.

Dave McMenamin. "Shots Heard 'Round the World." March 10, 2010. http://sports.espn.go.com/los-angeles/nba/columns/ story?id=4983889.

Dave McMenamin. "Unfounded Stigma Still Following Bryant." May 17, 2010. http://sports.espn.go.com/los-angeles/nba/col umns/story?id=5195953.

NBA.com. "Eighty-One! Bryant Erupts as Lakers Roll." January 22, 2006. wwww.nba.com/games/20060122/TORLAL/recap .html.

NBC Sports. "Kobe Accuser's Credibility Under Fire." December 17, 2003. http://nbcsports.msnbc.com/id/3723073.

Allison Samuels. "Who Is the Real Kobe." *Newsweek*, July 28, 2003. www.newsweek.com/2003/07/27/who-is-the-real-kobe.print.html.

Bill Saporito. "Kobe Rebounds." *Time*, September 13, 2004. www.time.com/time/magazine/article/0,9171,995069,00 .html.

Mark Starr. "The Laker Wars." *Newsweek*, July 1, 2004. www .newsweek.com/2004/06/30/the-laker-wars.html.

Ian Thomsen. "Showtime!" *Sports Illustrated*, April 27, 1998. http://sportsillustrated.cnn.com/vault/article/magazine/ MAG1012689/index.htm.

Justin Verrier. "Before They Were Stars: Kobe Bryant." June 1, 2010. http://sports.espn.go.com/nba/playoffs/2010/columns/ story?page=beforetheywerestars-kobe-100601.

Royce Webb. "Kobe Makes Records Wilt." January 23, 2006. http://sports.espn.go.com/nba/dailydime?page=daily dime-060123.

Jeff Zillgitt. "Man on a Mission: Bryant Revels in Victory, Finals MVP." *USA Today*, June 16, 2009. www.usatoday.com/sports/ basketball/nba/2009-06-15-bryant-finals-mvp_N.htm.

Websites

KB24MVP.com (www.kb24mvp.com). The official website for Kobe Bryant offers the latest information on his career.

"Kobe Bryant Biography," Famous People Biography (www .famouspeoplebiographyguide.com/athlete/Kobe-bryant/ Kobe-Bryant-Biography.html). This website contains a profile of Bryant's life, a timeline, photographs, and other information on the Lakers star.

Los Angeles Lakers (www.nba.com/lakers). For the latest information on Bryant's professional team, this website is the best source.

National Basketball Association (www.nba.com/playerfile/kobe_bryant). The NBA's official website offers the complete statistics for Bryant's professional career, photographs, biography, and game descriptions.

Sports Illustrated **Scrapbook** (http://sportsillustrated.cnn.com/basketball/nba/features/2000/kobe_bryant/kobe_intro). The sports magazine provides articles and photographs about Bryant, going back to his high school career.

O'Neal, Shaquille, 27, 49, 75,
   75, 85
   in 1999 NBA Finals, 44
   benching of, 54
   feud between Kobe and, 33,
      37, 38, 42
   on Kobe's winning NBA player
      of the decade, 85
   leaves LA Lakers, 70

P
Payton, Gary, 67
Philadelphia 76ers, 20
Phoenix Suns, 78
Popovich, Gregg, 79
Portland Trail Blazers, 44
Product endorsements, 64, 65

R
Rambis, Kurt, 38
Reid, J. R., 38
Rice, Glenn, 38
Robertson, Oscar, 14
Rodman, Dennis, 38
Ruckriegle, Terry, 61, 63
Rush, Kareem, 59
Russell, Bill, 75, 79

S
Sacramento Kings, 52
Salley, John, 42, 47
San Antonio Spurs, 40, 56
Schwartz, Rob, 22

Scott, Byron, 33
Sexual assault charge, 59–63
Shaw, Brian, 16, 52, 74
Smith, Dean, 24
Stockton, John, 38
Stoute, Steve, 64

T
Tomjanovich, Rudy, 70, 72, 73
Triangle offense, 41
2002–2003 season, 54–56
2003–2004 season, 67–69
2004–2005 season, 70–73
2005–2006 season, 74, 76,
   78–79
2006–2007 season, 79, 81
2007–2008 season, 82–84, 86
2008–2009 season, 87–89
2009–2010 season, 89–90,
   92–93
2010–2011 season, 93–95

U
Utah Jazz, 38

V
Vujacic, Sasha, 81

W
Wade, Dwayne, 86
West, Jerry, 26, 28, 39
Western Conference Player of
   the Week, 54

About the Author

John F. Wukovits is a retired junior high school teacher and writer from Trenton, Michigan, who specializes in history and biography. Besides biographies of Anne Frank, Jim Carrey, Michael J. Fox, Stephen King, and Martin Luther King Jr. for Lucent, he has written biographies of the World War II commander Admiral Clifton Sprague, Barry Sanders, Tim Allen, Jack Nicklaus, Vince Lombardi, and Wyatt Earp. He is also the author of many books about World War II, including the July 2003 book *Pacific Alamo: The Battle for Wake Island*, the August 2006 *One Square Mile of Hell: The Battle for Tarawa*, the November 2006 *Eisenhower: A Biography*, and the June 2009 volume *American Commando*, about marine colonel Evans Carlson and his Marine Raiders. A graduate of the University of Notre Dame, Wukovits is the father of three daughters—Amy, Julie, and Karen—and the grandfather of Matthew, Megan, Emma, and Kaitlyn.